Also by Elisha Cooper

FOR ADULTS

A Year in New York

Off the Road: An American Sketchbook

A Day at Yale

Henry: A Dog's Life

California: A Sketchbook

*Ridiculous, Hilarious, Terrible, Cool:
A Year in an American High School*

Crawling: A Father's First Year

FOR CHILDREN

Country Fair

Ballpark

Building

Dance!

Ice Cream

Magic Thinks Big

Bear Dreams

A Good Night Walk

Beach

Beaver Is Lost

Farm

Homer

Train

8: An Animal Alphabet

FALLING

FALLING

———— ∾ ————

A Daughter, a Father,
and a Journey Back

Elisha Cooper

Pantheon Books

New York

All rights reserved. Published in the United States by
Pantheon Books, a division of Penguin Random House LLC,
New York, and distributed in Canada by Random House
of Canada, a division of Penguin Random House Canada
Limited, Toronto.

Pantheon Books and colophon are registered trademarks of
Penguin Random House LLC.

Library of Congress Cataloging-in-Publication Data
Name: Cooper, Elisha.
Title: Falling : a daughter, a father, and a journey back /
Elisha Cooper.
Description: First edition. New York : Pantheon, 2016.
Identifiers: LCCN 2015042319. ISBN 9781101871232
(hardcover). ISBN 9781101871249 (ebook).
Subjects: LCSH: Cooper, Elisha. Authors, American—
20th century—Biography. Illustrators—United States—
Biography. Fathers and daughters—United States—
Biography. Cancer—Patients—Biography. BISAC:
BIOGRAPHY & AUTOBIOGRAPHY/Personal Memoirs.
BIOGRAPHY & AUTOBIOGRAPHY/Artists, Architects,
Photographers. FAMILY & RELATIONSHIPS/Parenting/
Fatherhood.
Classification: LCC PS3553.O5823 Z46 2016.
DDC 818/.603—dc23. LC record available at
lccn.loc.gov/2015042319

www.pantheonbooks.com

Jacket illustration by the author
Jacket design by Janet Hansen

Printed in the United States of America
First Edition

9   8   7   6   5   4   3   2   1

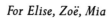

For Elise, Zoë, Mia

CONTENTS

It   3

Fall   12

Scans   26

Art   36

Family   44

Waiting   56

Words   67

Table   76

Orchard   86

Cycling   95

Wild   102

Williamsburg   110

Remember   117

Contents

Laughter   124

Thanks   133

And   138

Acknowledgments   145

FALLING

It

———— ✑ ————

It starts like this. I am picking up my daughter from day camp on the shores of Lake Michigan and taking her to Wrigley Field. Zoë likes the Cubs, so I thought I would surprise her with a game. It's a pretty day, and as we bike along the brownstone streets of Chicago's Lakeview neighborhood, my daughter on the bike seat behind me with her curly hair blowing in the wind, we are the vision of summer.

We enter the crowd and I buy two tickets behind home plate. Zoë is almost five, small for her age, so she sits on my lap so she can see better. As the game starts, I throw my left arm around her body, my hand cupping her side, and there, under her ribs, I feel a bump.

I don't make much of it, though at night I mention it to Elise. It feels like an extra rib, though there isn't one on her right side. Neither of us is concerned; nevertheless, in the morning I make an appointment with our pediatrician, just to be safe. The next day I take Zoë to the pediatrician, who feels Zoë's side and says the bump is probably a cyst, and will go away, though the following day it feels bigger.

On Saturday we go to another game at Wrigley Field, this time with Elise and Zoë's little sister, Mia. The Cubs lose, as they do, but everyone has a good time and we take a family photo next to the field after the game. As a precaution we had scheduled an ultrasound, so on Monday morning Elise brings Zoë and Mia to a nearby imaging clinic. Elise is finishing her postdoc in Chicago and will start teaching at NYU in the fall. We are moving to New York in two weeks.

I write children's books and have to sketch an illustration this morning for my next book. My desk in our second-floor apartment looks over a quiet street of brownstones and shaded trees, and I am standing next to my desk, sharpening my pencil and staring out the window when the phone rings. It's Elise, and her voice is quiet, and she is saying there is a tumor on Zoë's kidney and I am watching the leaves outside the window turn in the morning light, waving and bobbing in the breeze— tumor, kidney, kidney, tumor—and I listen to Elise, and I don't think the word "cancer" is said by either of us, and it's such a pretty day, and then I am out the door.

We meet at the edge of our local park, Elise coming toward me with the girls in their jogger. We hold each other, and I give each of my daughters a kiss on her head—they are happily playing with each other—and Elise and I hold each other again.

4

The next days are blurry, but everything we do is very precise. We call our pediatrician. We arrange to meet the oncologist. We go to Children's Memorial Hospital across the park and meet the oncologist, a smiling man with small glasses. He tells us Zoë has a pediatric kidney cancer called Wilms' tumor, a "good cancer," a funny pairing of words. Surgery is scheduled, as soon as possible, two days from now. We meet the surgeon, who shows us on a monitor the tumor surrounding Zoë's kidney. It's a dark mass, unreadable. We make more phone calls. Parents, insurers. When one of us is on the phone, the other is with the girls. Our minds are never where we are.

Elise calls NYU and tells them we have to delay our move to New York. I call the publicist for a book I wrote about being a father—the paperback is coming out next month—and tell her I won't be able to do all the things I said I was going to do. I hear in her silences she doesn't know what to say. I call friends back east. I reach one as he's driving to the city from Fire Island and in the background I hear seagulls.

We go to a beach on the lake with Zoë and some of her friends. As the girls play in the water, we talk with the parents, keeping our voices level with nothing-to-see-here expressions on our faces. At night we tell Zoë the growth on her kidney needs to come out, and how that will happen, and that everything will be okay. Zoë looks at us and nods. We tell Mia that her sister needs to go to the doctor and that everything will be okay. Mia nods too, like her sister. We take baths. On Zoë's left side we are able to see the tumor now. In two days it has grown and is rearing out from under her ribs, like something inside punching outward. We sit on the couch and tell bedtime stories.

Once the girls are asleep we call friends who are doctors, and at midnight we read and reread the Mayo Clinic website, our apartment illuminated by the soft glow of computer screens. Numbers and percentages, probabilities of survival. Numbers that, once learned, we will never not know. We are experts now. We know the numbers.

Then we shut down our computers and lie in bed.

Zoë's day camp is in a church across the street from Children's Memorial. On Thursday we pick Zoë up. She's wearing her nursery school T-shirt. The drawing of the child on the shirt looks like Zoë, with its curly hair and small smile. She looks no different than she did last week. We bring her stuffed tiger, and we walk across the street.

Hours of drinking fluids and fasting, reading books in the bright light of the waiting room. Plastic chairs circle the room, and down one corridor comes a distal hum. Empty halls seem to lead everywhere. Then it is time, and as Zoë is led away by a nurse through a swinging door we tell her we will see her very soon.

We wait. An hour, five hours. The surgery takes longer than it is supposed to—a soundless television with breaking news hangs from the ceiling above us—then we are summoned and meet the surgeon in a windowless room. The surgeon looks tired. There were complications, the tumor broke apart. The surgeon removed the tumor, and the kidney, and had to remove part of the colon, too. The cancer is stage three, which is not good. But I am not thinking about that and we are led to Zoë, and we are able to see her, and she's asleep. So peaceful and so pretty, her head resting on her stuffed tiger, tubes spiraling out of her.

I don't remember when she woke, I don't remember when I went to bed. In the next days Elise and I are always with her, or shuttling home to be with Mia. We take turns, though at night it is mostly Elise. We set up camp in Zoë's room in the hospital. During the day we go to the playroom, Zoë rolling on the stand that holds her IV and wearing a green gown that covers the horizontal stitches on her side. We bring Mia to visit. She clambers onto her sister's bed. They share pancakes.

The days are hot, the evenings cool, and at midnight I bike through empty streets to the hospital, though it is only two blocks away. I try to sleep on the chair at Zoë's side. At four in the morning we are woken by a pack of white-coated residents who watch us from behind clipboards. After six days, Zoë comes home.

The next week we bike downtown to Northwestern Memorial Hospital for radiation. The radiologist is round and South Asian and friendly. His four assistants draw on Zoë's belly, measuring to the millimeter, in blue ink. Then she is slid flat into the radiation machine. Zoë's stuffed tiger goes in the machine, too.

"It's all in the biology," says the radiologist as we wait in a control room bleeping with screens, giving me a big grin. Everyone here is so cheerful.

On the bike ride home Zoë throws up. We don't hear her at first. She's tough, the kind of child who doesn't want people to see her cry. In the next weeks she has nine more radiation treatments, and she starts chemotherapy. We have more appointments at Children's Memorial. We call doctors at Memorial Sloan Kettering in New York. We call doctors at New York-Presbyterian. We meet our oncologist. He tells us Zoë's histology is good, though I'm not exactly sure what that means. We plan our daughter's treatment and the continuing chemotherapy she will receive in the fall.

"It's going to be okay," the oncologist says before we leave the last time, giving me a hearty handshake.

Is it?

What is "it"? This unspoken it. But we know what it is. It is everything, and it is all in the biology, and it is what we have become, and we would think more about it but we have a birthday party to plan.

We had to cancel Zoë's birthday party when she was in the hospital, so now we plan a shared birthday party for her and Mia. Elise bakes a cake with butterflies and bugs in the frosting and our friends gather in the local park. The day is humid and we lead the girls and their friends on a scavenger hunt through Oz Park, following clues we taped to the statue of the Cowardly Lion and the Scarecrow. Then we eat pizza in the shade. Just another festive, manic birthday party, interrupted by a dog stealing the pizza. But even that doesn't matter and the girls blow out the candles. Zoë is five. Mia is three.

We slice the cake, and afterward the children go to the playground with Elise as I clean up, and here's that dog again, a silvery Weimaraner, and this time he's going for the cake.

What the hell? I look around for the dog's owner and see him standing to the side in shades and a button-down shirt.

"Hey, watch your fucking dog," I say.

The man tells me to watch my language, tells me that children are present, tells me something about his being a lawyer, but I am reaching for a piece of cake.

Throwing a piece of cake is not easy, especially one covered with frosting. As the piece of cake flies through the air—my throw underhanded and weak—I think about that second baseman who played for the New York Yankees a few years ago and couldn't make the simplest throw to first base, and the piece comes down halfway between me and the man, splattering the ground.

"I'm a lawyer!" the man shouts. "I'm a *lawyer!*"

Something about his emphasis makes me reach for a second piece. This time my throw is better and the man grabs his Weimaraner and runs. As I stand watching him go, one hand smeared in chocolate and the other, I realize, holding a frosting-covered kitchen knife, I wonder if there are elements of this story that may get away from me.

We pack up our apartment. Boxes of books, pots and pans, the original art from my own books. I drive out to DeKalb County to the farm I've been sketching for my next children's book and tell the farmer I will return in the fall. I bike to the café across from the old movie theater in Lincoln Square where I wrote the book about first becoming Zoë's father. We pack our desks, fitting everything we own into the orange-ribboned U-Haul parked out front that will go to New York before us. I take trips up and down the stairs, as Zoë and Mia play in a water sprinkler on the sidewalk out front.

Our last weekend in Chicago we go again to Wrigley Field. We sit near first base, so close to home we can hear the smack of the ball into the catcher's mitt. Our seats are not far from where Zoë and I sat last month, the difference between that day and this day so large it resists metaphor. We move from before to after; we have no idea what will come. All we know is that everything is different and that we must go.

Zoë gets tired and we leave early, though not before a player from the other team launches a ball deep into the bleachers and we see the ball thrown back. In the morning we will be gone.

After a last look around our empty apartment, and

a last wave to our street, we pack into our blue station wagon—Elise beside me in the front, Mia in the backseat with her sheep blanket, Zoë with her stuffed tiger—and we head south along Lake Michigan, the skyline slipping away from us in the rearview mirror.

We drive away on a beautiful day in late summer, me and my girls.

Good-bye, Chicago.

Fall

———— ❦ ————

Our new home is on the seventh floor of a large building south of Washington Square Park. It's faculty housing, ugly and brick, but in the heart of Greenwich Village. Our corner apartment is white walled and modern, with windows and a small balcony just above the tree line, so it feels like we're in a tree house, or the prow of a boat cutting through a green ocean. From our kitchen we can look across the street into our neighbors' kitchen; they can look into ours.

Friends come and help. College friends, and friends from when we used to live in New York. Someone brings pizza and we eat on the floor among unpacked boxes. My childhood friend Barney brings ice cream. Another friend gives Zoë and Mia ten dollars each to root for the Mets. Our friends rally around us. As they leave they say, "Let us know if there's anything we can do."

But most of what we do we do alone. Unpacking boxes, building bookshelves, assembling a bunk bed, hooking up the Internet, having a dishwasher installed.

Then we tuck the girls into bed and fill out school forms, details carrying us into the night.

We count down the days to Zoë's first day of kindergarten and then, inevitably, that morning is here. We walk through Washington Square Park under the marble arch, then north on Fifth Avenue and west on Eleventh Street, joining a stream of families that pools in front of Public School 41. Parents anxious and beaming, children anxious. The doors open and we step inside, Zoë's kindergarten teacher greeting everyone with an impossibly animated smile. Zoë stares at her. Zoë is wearing a light blue dress and sits with Elise at a small desk, lightly holding Elise's ear—something she did when she was an infant—and then we go.

Elise starts teaching. She's an assistant professor of applied psychology at NYU and her days fill with classes and meetings, and early morning runs along the river. I stay home and organize our apartment and set up my desk. Mostly I make deliveries and pickups. Delivering Mia to preschool, delivering Zoë to school, picking up Mia for lunch and a nap, then picking up Zoë. I find a café near PS 41 with good hot chocolate where we read after school. Then we walk home through Washington Square Park. We feel our way into the neighborhood, establishing routine.

Then, Friday. Friday is the day we go to the hospital.

In the week we are unpacking, we take the subway up to Washington Heights. New York-Presbyterian sits on the ridge of Upper Manhattan, looking out over the Hudson River. A clunky cluster of brick buildings mimicked by the hospital's clunky name—New York-Presbyterian, Morgan Stanley Children's Hospital, Columbia University Medical Center, Herbert Irving Pavilion, Herbert Irving Child and Adolescent Oncology Center. After a while we refer to all of it as "the hospital."

At the Herbert Irving Pavilion we get a pass from the security guard and ride the elevator to the seventh floor and the pediatric oncology clinic. The reception room is awash in pastels. Stenciled turtles and fish and ladybugs swim around the floor in greens and blues. The receptionists are welcoming and friendly, slipping an ID band around Zoë's wrist and giving us multiple forms to fill out. Then we wait for Dr. Alice Lee.

We hear her first, a *click-clack* of high heels. As she turns the corner her smile precedes her, too. She says hello to Zoë, leaning down and sort of ignoring us. Young and animated, with black hair angling over an open and affable face, she wears a soft white sweater. Her kindness and directness are instantly assuring—something Elise sensed when they spoke on the phone from Chicago—along with the fact that Dr. Alice Lee is an expert on Wilms' tumor.

We plan the fall. Every Friday, Zoë will come to the hospital. She will come with me, or with Elise. She will be weighed and measured, have her blood taken and sent to the lab for its white-blood-cell count, then have dactinomycin or vincristine or doxorubicin drip through the port that had been inserted in her chest during surgery and into her body. Twenty-two weeks of chemotherapy. Everything leading to CT scans in the winter that will tell us whether all this—surgery to remove the tumor, radiation to kill remaining cancer cells, chemotherapy to keep remaining cancer cells killed—has worked. That is the plan.

After talking with Dr. Lee about the details—and also about her favorite foods and favorite musicals as she and Zoë chat together on the examining table—we thank her and walk out of the hospital into a bright and beautiful morning.

A few years ago, on a similar beautiful fall morning, Elise and I woke up at my friend Barney's apartment in Greenwich Village. We were in New York for a wedding, having flown in from California, where Elise was in grad school at Berkeley. Barney's shower was broken so we put on our clothes from the night before and walked over to West Fourth Street and caught the A train to JFK, which took us beneath the World Trade Center at the same time the first plane hit the north tower above us.

We had no idea. We came out the other side—a man in our subway car pointed out the smoking tower behind us as we rolled through Brooklyn—and we reached the airport and turned around and took a livery cab to Elise's grandmother's apartment in Bay Ridge. We could see the tops of both towers billowing in the distance, a pair of out-of-place smokestacks, and then we couldn't. We called our family—they were frantic because they knew we were flying to California that morning—then our cell phones gave out and we walked through Brooklyn to the river. As we walked past Green-Wood Cemetery, there were small birds pecking at seeds in the grass and flitting up into the trees, back and forth, and sometimes a piece of paper, burned at its edges, would flutter down next to the birds. I picked up one of these, a memo from the Secret Service from an office in the towers. In the air above us I could see a contrail of other papers flying eastward. Shimmery and white in the blue sky, they looked like migrating birds.

For the next week, with no flights out of New York, we were stranded. We crossed back to the Village—the void to the south of us smoking and reeking—and met friends and gave water to firefighters as they roared up and down the West Side Highway. We read newspapers, and MISSING notices in parks, and in the afternoon we gave more water. Mostly we walked the deserted streets of Downtown and felt there was little we could do.

When I think of those days I remember two things. The color of the sky that morning, that cerulean blue. How clear it was. How strange that on such a beautiful day, birds could be flying in one part of the city while tragedy unfolded in another. How there could be so much beauty in the world, and so much horror, blocks from each other. How normality and madness could coexist.

I also remember waking in Brooklyn that first night. In my hazy three-in-the-morning state I wondered if what had happened had happened and then I smelled that acrid smell through the window and knew that yes, it had. It took an hour to fall asleep. The next night I woke, and the next, but each time the smell wasn't as sharp and I returned to sleep earlier, and then I didn't wake until daybreak. Shock dulled into day-to-day. But what didn't change was change. There was the sense that the world was realigned, there was no going back. Life was propulsive.

I guess there's a last thing I remember: Elise and I felt like New Yorkers again. We had lived in the city before, and like many we were affected but not directly. We were witnesses. With all the clamor from the rest of the country, the attack made us feel isolated. New York was alone, no one understood. We would have to figure this out and move forward by ourselves. After a week we flew home to California and Elise was pregnant within a month. Sometimes I think that September morning led directly to Zoë.

The fall continues. During the day I shop for groceries or do publicity work I was supposed to do for the paperback of my fatherhood book. I sign copies of the book at bookstores. I introduce myself to the owner of Three Lives & Company, our local bookstore, and convince him to put the book in the window (on the back cover there's a photo of Zoë and me, her staring into the camera with big one-year-old eyes). I go to a café in the Village and check proofs of an upcoming children's book and drink too many macchiatos. Afterward I take the subway to the offices of *The New Yorker* magazine, where I used to work, and meet editors I used to work for. On my way downtown I look at my reflection in a window of the F train and see a dried band of coffee foam across my nose, which had been there the whole time. I pick the girls up from school and tell them this story at dinner.

Mornings bring their first chill. We look down to the street to see what pedestrians are wearing and dress accordingly. We dress Zoë in clothes that mothers in her kindergarten class have given to us: a soft white vest, a furry brown hat. The mothers are so generous. It is unsaid but we are known at the school as the new family with the girl with cancer.

Some days it rains, and while Mia naps outside in the jogger, I send Zoë into the café for hot chocolates. I give her a twenty-dollar bill; sometimes she doesn't bring back the change. As we walk home I tell the girls about the Minetta Stream running underneath where cabs now whoosh up Sixth Avenue. Or I point out the brownstone where Mark Twain lived. We walk through the park past the statue of Giuseppe Garibaldi. We wave at him and come home to the smell of sautéing onions. Barney comes over, and as Elise and I cook, the girls chase him around the apartment, tugging at his long legs. During dinner, Zoë and Mia tell us what they did at school today, the friends they are making. Afterward I clean up and watch them on the couch—Mia with her sheep blanket, Zoë with her tiger—leaning into Elise as she reads aloud. Then baths and bedtime. The normality of a week.

But every week has a Friday.

The security guard at the Herbert Irving Pavilion recognizes us and waves us through. The receptionists at the clinic give us smiles and loop an ID band around Zoë's ankle so her hands are free to draw. Nurses give her hugs and take her blood. They are kind and careful, and as they ask Zoë what she's learned at school this week while attaching the needle to the line for the doxorubicin, the action takes on a slightly dissonant air, like someone singing a lullaby while loading a gun.

Zoë does not cry. Sometimes she narrows her eyes, a small stoic (when told not to move in the radiation machine at Northwestern she lay motionless for twenty minutes). We sit in comfortable chairs and watch as the salmon-colored liquid drips down a bendy tube and into her. I read books to her, and out our window we can see tugboats and barges sliding up and down the Hudson. After an hour the nurses check to see how much doxorubicin remains and make Zoë promise to bring her stuffed tiger in next week so they can be properly introduced. Then we hear heels coming down the hall, and Dr. Lee is ready to see us. She asks Zoë what's new in kindergarten while listening to her chest with a stethoscope, her patter never stopping, palpating her belly with searching fingers, the smile never leaving her face. Four hours after we entered the hospital, we are free to go. We head outside loaded down with so many toys it looks like we robbed a toy store and we slip back into the city, back into the world of the unbanded.

Some Fridays after the hospital I bring Zoë back to school. Most Fridays she is tired and when we get off at West Fourth Street I carry her to 'Ino, an Italian restaurant on Bedford Street where we share small sandwiches. We pick Mia up from preschool, then go to the café. Mia naps in the jogger, Zoë buys hot chocolate. She's known as the "big-tipping girl" now and the baristas change the name of the chocolate on the chalkboard: THE LITTLE ZOË.

The days grow short. I fly back to Chicago to sketch the corn harvest for my children's book on farms. I rent a car and drive out to DeKalb County and meet the farmer in his field under a wide midwestern sky. The corn was green when I was here last but has turned yellow and dusty. I climb into the cab of his combine and it roars back and forth, eating up stalks and pumping a stream of golden seeds into the hopper behind us. The farmer tells me that sometimes a fox gets caught in front of the combine and the exhausted animal just keeps running until the combine turns at the end of the row. I drive into the city and walk by our old home, then around Children's Memorial. As I head through the park I see the lawyer and his Weimaraner. I can't believe it. Where is a slice of cake when you need one? But he does not recognize me and I don't say anything and keep going and fly back to New York.

The days grow windy. The ocean of trees outside our window has turned brown. Leaves whip our legs as we walk to school. For Halloween, both girls are butterflies. Elise sews wings to the backs of flowered dresses. We join the parade around Washington Square Park, with Zoë sitting on my shoulders. At night, one of Elise's students comes over and stays with the girls as they sleep and Elise and I go out to dinner. We talk about friends and work and family. We talk about our new life here. But there are times when we just hold hands and don't say anything. There's not much to say we both don't know.

We keep moving.

Over Thanksgiving we drive to the farm in Connecticut where I grew up. When I was a boy we had goats and horses and cats, but those are gone, buried at the crest of the orchard. My parents have two old dogs now. Zoë and Mia climb on them and climb the apple trees. We hike through the lower fields, the ground brittle with frost, and come inside to a table filled with turkey and bread, and vegetables from my parents' garden.

Back in the city, the evenings are dark and bright with Christmas tree lights. The season of holiday parties, and we go to a party at a friend's place in Brooklyn. Mia wears a dark blue velvet dress, Zoë's dress is red. They are playing in front of a fireplace.

I leave them for a moment to get food, and as I am returning with two plates, I look across the room through this swirling and happy crowd and see Zoë and stop.

Who is this girl? She looks ill. This is an ill girl. From this distance she looks so small and so thin. Her arms are bones, her arms are clothes hangers inside her dress. Her hair wisps her head. Her eyes, which were large before, are if possible even larger, wide and luminous in her gaunt face. Her eyes are immense.

Anyone would see this but us. We can't see this. Since we see her every day, since she is right in front of us, we don't see the change in her. But, then, how would we see her differently? Because this is Zoë. This is my daughter, we are doing everything we always do, she is playing with her sister, some inimitable game of their own devising, and I am bringing them food.

But the convergence of these feelings, at this party in Brooklyn brimming with warmth, looking from this remove at my daughter who may or may not still have cancer, who may or may not have a new tumor, who has undergone months of chemotherapy the success of which we do not know, and the possibility of what we will find in her scans this winter and what that would mean, this gutting knowledge enters me and leaves me . . .

I don't think about it. I do not think about it.

All I know is that tomorrow we will wake up and get dressed and eat breakfast. We will walk across the park to school, and in the afternoon we will go to the café and drink hot chocolate. Our bodies will take over and we will lose our minds in books and we will come home for dinner and laugh and take baths and read more books and tuck our children into bed and in the morning we will wake up and do it again. We will keep moving. Tomorrow and the tomorrow after that. The unavoidable velocity of a day.

When I was in college, I spent a summer out west working for the U.S. Forest Service. I was in a trail crew building fences in the Salmon National Forest, up in the mountains of the Continental Divide on the border between Idaho and Montana. The trail crew was made up of a bunch of silent men and led by a silent Vietnam vet. I was the talkative kid from back east.

One of the silent men had a set of weights in his basement—he told us he was the dead-lift champion of Idaho—and since I was getting in shape for the upcoming football season, I would go to his house after work each day to lift. His house was at the bottom of the Lemhi Valley, twenty miles from the Forest Service station where I was staying. Some days I would bike there, work out for an hour, then bike back. Some days I hitched a ride down the valley in a pickup, my bicycle in the bed of the truck.

One day I caught a ride with the Forest Service biologist on the back of his motorcycle.

The biologist had a mustache that made him look like a marauding Viking. His motorcycle was a black Harley. He told me just to hold my bicycle, that this would be okay, no problem, so I hopped on behind him and held my bike over my shoulder and threw my other arm around his waist. I can't remember now if I wore a helmet. I don't think I did.

We started down the road, gathering speed as we accelerated past ranches and high desert scrub, carving the bends of the willow-lined Lemhi River at fifty miles an hour, sixty, seventy. We cut the wind. The Harley roared, the biologist's mustache reaching back to me on either side of his face in whipping auburn tendrils. Sometimes he would shout something and I would shout something back to make it seem like I had heard. Or he would point out a detail on the valley's horizon and I would watch his hand and wait for him to put it back on the handlebar.

As we flew down the valley—my bike against my back, my arm around this biologist I did not know—I got the sense that this was not wise. That this was quite possibly the most dangerous thing I had ever done. Ludicrous, insane.

But there wasn't anything to do about it. Or, at least, getting off didn't feel like an option. My fear was so immediate the only thing to do was suspend it, or give in to it. Giving in or not was not even the point, just making it around the next bend was, and the bend after that, as the farms and ditches of the Lemhi Valley swept past in a wilding blur. I held on as tight as I could and leaned into the curves, embracing the impossible in an act of faith as we sped down the road in front of us.

Scans

———— ✑ ————

We are eating peanut butter and jelly sandwiches in the reception room of the pediatric oncology clinic. I'm sitting sideways on a couch. Zoë is straddling the back of the couch, up against the window. From here we can watch pedestrians scurrying along Fort Washington Avenue, hunched against the wind in their puffy winter coats, the plumes of their breath billowing into the cold air. It's a nice place for a picnic.

"That's dangerous," says a voice behind me. "She can't sit there."

I turn and there's a doctor. I don't recognize him, though later I'll learn he's the head of the department. I tell him we are fine, that we're just sitting here eating our lunch, that my daughter is safe.

"No. That's dangerous," the doctor repeats. "She could get hurt."

He stands to the side, arm outstretched like a maître d' guiding us away from our table. So I gather our sandwiches and lift Zoë off the couch and we retreat across the room. Zoë asks why we have to move and I mumble something about safety, trying to sound like it's no big deal.

But inside I am seething. Eating a sandwich on top of a couch is dangerous? Sitting against a window is dangerous? Are you kidding me? *Cancer* is dangerous. Cancer *kills* people.

In two weeks Zoë will have her post-treatment CT scans. These are the critical scans, the ones that will answer the questions: Did surgery work, did radiation work, did twenty-two weeks of chemotherapy work. Is she cancer free?

But I am not thinking about that right now. I am thinking I should have said something to that doctor. I am composing an angry little speech. I will walk up to the front desk and complain! I will tell them my philosophy of risk.

I grew up with a relaxed view of risk. Or, a rural view. When I was eight I put a saddle on my brother's back and rode him around our kitchen. This kitchen rodeo lasted about three seconds. Now I have a large cap on my front tooth, which has yellowed with age. But I think of my busted tooth as a good reminder. Sometimes you break a tooth but sometimes you learn to ride your brother. More importantly, if you never fall you will fall off something higher later and probably fall harder.

My brother and I lived this falling philosophy. We fell off our ponies, fell off hay-bale forts we built in the loft of the barn, and when we were older I tumbled out the open door of my brother's jeep as he swerved around the muddy lower fields. But we bounced back. Friends from New Haven came out to our farm and really hurt themselves. They fell out of trees and broke their legs (my parents, amazingly, were never sued). I think I knew even then that familiarity made me safe. I would visit friends in New Haven and trip on the sidewalk.

Parents in my generation often look back on their "we biked everywhere" childhoods with nostalgia. Then they instill a "you can't bike anywhere" philosophy in their own children. This is especially true of urban educated parents, who worry about all the awful possibilities—abducted kids, speeding taxis—then put their children in a bubble. Safety becomes *the* goal. Risk is risky. Which is why ever since coming to New York we have been climbing trees.

On the west side of Central Park, in the shadow of the American Museum of Natural History, is a large gnarled beech tree. In the fall we came to the park every other weekend. I'd feed Zoë and Mia into the tree's branches, then stand underneath as they swung above me and try to ignore various horrified old ladies and their small dogs as they barked: "*What* are those girls doing up there?!"

Inevitably a park ranger would roll up in his cruiser and make the girls climb down. So we'd head downtown and climb trees in the park along the river until park rangers there made us climb down, too.

"It's not safe," they all said.

I never said anything back. But I thought the park rangers, and New York parents in general, had it backward. I thought it unsafe *not* to climb trees. Unsafe to be safe. Parents had taken common sense (seat belts in cars) and expanded it to make no sense (wearing helmets on push scooters). Parents' anxiety actually increased children's danger because children didn't know how to fall. Children needed more risk, not less. I wanted my children to walk by themselves to school, know how to use a jackknife, and fall out of trees (short trees) and get back up.

But what if my philosophy was wrong?

When Zoë was a toddler she was bitten by a dog. We were at a camp in Maine with old friends and their young dog. The dog bit Zoë on top of her head when she patted him. After we returned from the local clinic—a line of stitches on the part in Zoë's hair—the man who ran the camp offered to kill the dog. He didn't say how, though the expression on his face said he knew. He was the father of two girls and I think he understood what I felt in that moment. That I had failed to protect my child, failed as a father in some way, and was in need of some redemption.

We decided not to kill the dog, though I spent the following years swearing that next time I would be ready somehow. Next time I would protect my child. My response would be swift and murderous—though all it really left me with was a more tightly wound temper.

So I knew my philosophy had some contradiction. Wanting my daughters to take risks, but ready to attack anything that could harm them. Wanting my daughters to climb trees, but ready to fight anyone who would keep them from climbing. Wanting, paradoxically, to protect my daughters' right to be dangerous. Most of all, I wanted to act.

One dark night before the holidays, Zoë woke with a fever. She was clammy and pale, and running a fever while undergoing chemotherapy is serious, so Elise wrapped her in a blanket as I got our car, then I sped up the West Side Highway through blinking traffic lights and parked on Broadway and carried Zoë through the doors of the New York-Presbyterian emergency room. Emergency rooms in the early morning hours are taut and stressful, but as Zoë was hooked to an IV and color returned to her face, I sat by her side and felt so calm. Once the fever stabilized I drove us home. It was a Sunday morning, and as I walked down our hall I could smell the scones that Elise and Mia had baked and I entered our apartment with Zoë in my arms like some returning warrior. As if I had fought something and won.

That feeling wore off.

Because how do you fight cancer? How do you fight something you can't see? I would like to fight it, would like to fight something, or someone, but there is no enemy here and that leaves me swinging blindly, punching at air.

A few days after our trip to the emergency room I brought Zoë to the playground in front of our building. The ground was hard and icy. I was pushing Zoë on the tire swing, looping her through the air in parabolas, her furry brown hat skiddering inches above the pavement, when an adorable blond four-year-old girl from the building next door walked over and started to watch.

"Let's give Eva a turn," I said.

Zoë got out of the tire swing and helped the girl inside. Eva wrapped her arms around the tire and stared up at us. Could we push her? I asked. Could both girls swing together? Eva did not budge. She just stood there as Zoë and I presented the options (not so many with a tire swing), and I looked around for her parent but saw no one. The girl held tight, a blond barnacle.

As she stood inside the tire, glaring at us, I began to see this child not as a mere annoyance but as a small outrage. She was ruining our day in the park, harming my daughter, my daughter who was kind and had cancer and just wanted to swing free. But there was nothing to do about it and we walked away.

"Eva is being an asshole," I said. "Let's go climb some trees."

Back in the pediatric oncology clinic we have finished our peanut butter and jelly sandwiches. We have met Dr. Lee. On our way out of the hospital I stop at the front desk. I tell the receptionist about the doctor who made us leave the couch, then I start talking about risk, how risk is good, and how I was there to catch my child. In the receptionist's sympathetic face I can tell she has seen behavior like mine before and is letting me talk myself out. I know my words aren't clear, that I am swinging back and forth between questions that confuse me, and eventually my sentences sputter to a stop and I thank the receptionist for listening and we head for the elevator.

Two weeks later we are at the third-floor radiology department at New York-Presbyterian for Zoë's scans. The CT room is bright and white walled. The massive CT "donut" hums in the room's center. Zoë drinks a formula of fluid that lights her insides, then lies flat on the gurney, which slides her into the donut. Elise and I wait outside. Behind closed doors we hear clicks and whirrs. Twenty minutes later the scans are done and we are allowed back in. Through a pane of glass, we see a team of radiologists in the control room, huddled around a screen. I make small talk with a technician and ask her if we can draw on the white walls. She gives us Sharpies. I draw a bear, Zoë draws a castle, Elise draws two children holding hands. Then we walk back to the pediatric oncology clinic, where we wait another hour before Dr. Lee meets us and tells us the scans are clear.

We are sitting on a red couch in Dr. Lee's office. Dr. Lee is pointing at the grainy black-and-white image on her computer monitor, at the space where Zoë's kidney used to be, a space other organs have filled.

"She takes beautiful pictures," Dr. Lee says.

Elise is crying silently, trying not to make Zoë worry. Zoë has hopped up on the examining table and is telling Dr. Lee about *The Wizard of Oz,* lightly holding the hem of Dr. Lee's pink sweater. Dr. Lee looks into Zoë's ears with her otoscope and asks her what she will find in there (Dorothy in one ear, the Wicked Witch of the West in the other). Dr. Lee beams at Zoë as they talk, but she is beaming at us, too. There are two story lines in the room; the news today is very good. Here in this small room in this large hospital, the adults are on air. Elise and I walk out the door swinging Zoë between us.

We call our parents, we call our friends. We feel overwhelming relief. But in the next days this feeling starts to fade, in drips and drops and sliding increments, seeping away, and what fills the space is the knowledge that in three months we will be back at the hospital.

And three months after that, and after that. X-rays, ultrasounds, CT scans. These first scans were critical. Others will be critical, too. The two-year scans are the really important ones, the ones where the research on Wilms' tumor point to a child's survival. Or is it three years? I'm not exactly sure which year's scans are the most important.

And that might be the problem. Uncertainty stretches in front of us. The threat is gone. *The threat is not gone.*

Now we face years where we hope the cancer does not return. Now we wait. So within days of feeling such boundless relief, I just feel angry.

It's like we have been climbing a mountain and reached the summit only to realize that, no, it's a false summit, one of those deceptions of height where hidden trees and the tricks of topography mean there's another summit above us, and maybe another after that. So where is the real mountaintop, and where are we? We are standing on a trail, looking up and thinking we were done, but see that what should be ending is just beginning. Okay, that's over. Now what?

A late winter storm hits the city. Squalls of snow rattle our windows and I head with Zoë and Mia down to the basement to do laundry. The girls have brought a jump rope, and as I separate our clothes into the washers, Mia climbs into a wheeled metal laundry basket and holds one end of the rope as Zoë starts swinging her around the room. It's laundry room rodeo.

"That's dangerous," says a voice behind me. "They could get hurt."

I turn and see a woman with long gray hair.

"Oh, they're fine," I say as Zoë releases the rope and Mia in the laundry basket goes careering into a washer with a squeal of delight.

"Your daughters could get hurt!" the woman repeats.

She's drawn herself up in front of me, she wants me to make this stop. "They could end up in the hospital. *Really.*"

At this I rise up. I stick out my chin, trying the words on for size.

"Hey. My daughter has *cancer.*"

I start talking, the volume of my voice rising, cancer this, cancer that, how cancer is dangerous, how this woman doesn't know us, how she better *leave us alone,* and even as I say the words they feel ugly coming out of my mouth and I resolve never to use them again.

But as I am telling off this woman I see in her eyes that she—much like the receptionist at the hospital—is looking at a man who is a little unhinged. The protective parent, amplified. If this woman were particularly perceptive she might also see how scared the man in front of her is, but to recognize that would require an abundance of empathy, and as my words fall away from me all I know for certain is that I am alarming this woman. She gathers her laundry and walks away.

Zoë and Mia are now both inside the laundry basket, lying upside down and kicking their feet against the washers to propel themselves around the room, which, actually, does look a little dangerous.

I stand and watch. On my face is a smile, but inside I am on fire. I think I will remain here awhile, crashing around in the basement.

Art

———— ✑ ————

During the Great Depression my grandmother eloped with a Hungarian. They met in Cleveland and fell in love, but my grandmother's family didn't approve, so they fled in the middle of the night to New York and got married in Greenwich Village. The Hungarian's name was Stephen Starr. He had a mustache and a bulbous nose, one of which I inherited.

They lived in a brick row house on Morton Street, a few blocks west of where we live now. My grandfather worked an office job in the Empire State Building and went to NYU School of Law at night. My grandmother studied painting at the Art Students League. When they ate in their small kitchen they fashioned a table by resting her drawing board on top of their knees. A boy delivered eggs each morning, a man with a horse delivered milk by placing bottles in a basket lowered by pulley from their second-floor apartment. The rent was twenty-five dollars a month.

My grandmother painted an oil of their living room. It's a bright painting, with red curtains and open windows, the sun angling across the room and highlighting a pram. Outside, it looks like spring. The painting has a sense of beginnings, a new family starting out. The painting stayed with my grandparents when they moved to Morningside Heights after their rent went up to thirty dollars, then to Ohio when my mother was born. The painting now hangs at my uncle's house in California (he was the one in the pram) and is supposed to go to a museum near Cleveland when my grandmother dies.

My grandmother lives in an assisted-living community outside Philadelphia and paints less frequently now. When I was a child I remember watching her paint, her face a frown of concentration as she attacked the canvas. Decades of oil painting and chiseling marble sculptures have made her hands clenched and arthritic. She writes me letters though, sometimes including a shaky pencil sketch. She's ninety-nine. I send her my own art, rough drafts of whatever illustrations I'm working on.

It's spring and time to start painting my next children's book. But first, the café.

After walking Zoë to school I head to the same café I've been coming to since we moved to New York. Jack's is small, so small that sounds rattle around it like beans inside a mug: the *whrrrclunk* of the grinder, the *cack-cack-cack* of the espresso machine, the *hwwshh* of the milk steamer. I read *The New York Times* and watch people order lattes and give each other *sorry-I'm-late* hugs. The atmosphere of a café is important, since cafés are where I work.

I don't know many other children's book authors. I became friends with one named Kevin Henkes when I ran by his home in Madison, Wisconsin, with Zoë in a jogger (Elise grew up in Madison and we were visiting her old home). He and I write letters to each other now. When I won an award for a book about beaches (sketched on Lake Michigan with Zoë and Mia playing in the sand next to me), the head of the awards committee said my name wrong and took his shoe off and put it in his mouth, and I accepted the award in front of a roomful of strangers.

So I think of children's book authors as not only solitary, but awkward. More comfortable with paper and pencil than people. As I curl shavings from my pencil into a café saucer, I look through my sketchbooks and start crafting layouts. Fields and barns, tractors and chickens. Sometimes I look out the window at dogs and their walkers or sketch a barista when I'm thinking about a farmhand. Head in Illinois, eyes in New York, and everything merges. The people in the café, whether they know it or not, are my subjects and coworkers.

I head home to paint. The trees in Washington Square Park are blossoming pink, and when the wind picks up it's like walking in a pink snowstorm. As I walk I think how painting is reflection—how the atmosphere in a café and the weather outside affect the painting. This is also true for my internal atmosphere. Since I am thinking about Zoë's upcoming visit to the hospital for her first quarterly scans, I wonder how these paintings will turn out. What will come out on this paper?

At our apartment I take large sheaves of paper from under our bed, cut out a smaller piece, and tape that to my watercolor-stained wood desk. I turn on music, Green Day or the Shins, then change into shorts and a white T-shirt. I sit down in my chair with the loose screw that pokes into the back of my thighs, and with all my neuroses firmly in place, I begin.

As I draw my pencil across the surface, I realize I *know* this paper. Or my hand with its pencil knows the paper. How it responds sluggishly on a humid day, lightly when the temperature is cool. My fingers know how to rotate the pencil an imperceptible eighth of an inch so I can catch a new edge of graphite for my next stroke.

I am not professionally trained—I can't charcoal a nude or paint an oil—but I can make this pencil do what I want. Here, a rooster. Where I am drawing a rooster but I am really drawing the *idea* of a rooster, a two-inch-tall animal in eight dashes of pencil. It's not even a drawing but a two-dimensional gesture, an idea reaching from my hand to another's eyes. When I am drawing well I can give the rooster feeling—he's a little cocky—and sometimes I just watch this pencil in my hand move, and now there's a whole flock of roosters strutting across the paper.

I cut another piece and sketch a cornfield, then fill a glass with water and open my battered metal watercolor box and take a sable brush and layer shades of blue into the field, with shoots of green, and I sit at my desk and watch as the sun pours across the field and the shadows spread out from the barns and the farm takes shape.

Hours pass in minutes and now it is two o'clock and I forgot to eat lunch and have to pick up Mia and Zoë from school so I tape the paintings to the wall above my desk and stare at them.

During dinner, as the girls chatter about what they did at school today, my eyes wander over to the paintings. Sometimes, when everyone is sleeping, I slip out of bed and come back to my desk and turn on the light, bending its arm up and casting the paintings in sharp relief, noticing mistakes and thinking how I will correct them, but mostly I just stare and stare at the paintings and feel unmoored. Planetary.

Almost as if I were in the paintings. Or maybe the paintings are in me, or we are in some space flowing back and forth into each other, and as I keep working— the wall filling with clouds and fields and barns—I keep staring at these paintings and the more I look at them the more they seem sad to me and I wonder how that is possible.

I bring Zoë to the hospital for her first quarterly scans, an X-ray and an ultrasound, in the radiology department at NewYork-Presbyterian. The X-rays take minutes, the ultrasound stretches for hours, and afterward Zoë and I walk back to the pediatric oncology clinic and meet Dr. Lee in her office, where she tells us the scans are clear.

Dr. Lee and Zoë are talking about sushi. Zoë is trying to convince Dr. Lee that she should try sushi but meeting some resistance. Then they talk about where they would like to travel and agree on Italy.

As I listen to them, I feel the same relief I did three months ago. But, as I look at my daughter, something feels off. Not with her—her hair is growing back blond and curly, lighter than before, and every day she looks fuller and healthier—but with me. A feeling of detachment, as if I'm not completely here.

I am watching me watching her.

It's a sense of departure, but a sideways departure. More a feeling of being left behind. Maybe it's not that I am climbing a mountain where each summit reveals another summit above. Maybe I have stopped climbing altogether, and everyone else has gone ahead, and I have taken a turn into the wilderness, into the interior.

But these are not things I say to anyone. Dr. Lee tells us that the Make-A-Wish Foundation contacted her and would like to give Zoë a wish. So we throw around ideas: fly back to Chicago, see Zoë's old friends, see a show, maybe go to Wrigley Field and see the Cubs. We are touched and humbled by Make-A-Wish's generosity. Everyone in the room is smiling, and we walk out of the hospital into a beautiful spring day.

I have a book coming out this spring. I wrote it last year, before everything. It is irrelevant to me now. It's about eight students in a Chicago high school whom I followed through a year of adolescent drama and breakups and college applications. It has a dumb title.

I do all the normal things I do when I publish a book, but my heart's not in it. I fly to Chicago for a book festival, book signings, bookstore visits. With my obligations done I go for punishing runs along Lake Michigan that leave my right ankle throbbing. I cool off in the lake.

Elise and the girls fly out and join me. Make-A-Wish puts us up in a fancy hotel downtown. In the evening a limo carries us to the theater where we see *Wicked*. The orchestra swells and Zoë and Mia perch spellbound at the edge of their seats. The next day we take the L up to Wrigley Field and sit behind home plate. Make-A-Wish has thought of everything.

At night we have dinner with our Chicago friends—it's the first time we have all been together since we left last summer—and everyone is so happy to see one another. Everyone says how great Zoë looks. They ask how we are doing and we say we are fine. We are fine! Elise holds hands with the mothers and I give bear hugs to the fathers. I have the suspicion though that I am smiling more than usual. And I feel that same detachment I had when I was last in the hospital, more attuned to a small heartbeat of fear growing inside me: *here, not here, here, not here.*

Falling

I think about something Dr. Lee said when I was alone with her. I asked what recurrence would mean, and Dr. Lee, in the only time I have seen her not smile, said it would not be good. Recurrence means death. I know this. I have always known this. So as I look at my daughter now, and at my family, I just float away and I wonder if art can save me and I think about the paintings at home on my walls.

We fly back to New York and I throw myself into my painting. I am deep in the book now, down in the furrows of it. After dropping off the girls at school, I come home and cut paper and I tape it to my desk. I turn on music and take off my shoes and sharpen my pencil. I draw my way out of New York, away from its crowded streets, and back to the farms of the Midwest. I take my pencil and transport myself forward in time. It is fall there, and the rows of corn have been harvested, and I take my brush and layer washes of blue shadow into the soil and in the distance I paint low hills, with the sky gray and the sun trying to break through the clouds. I paint myself there. I paint myself up into the sky and down into the ground. There is a house and a barn, and a boy and a girl, a dog waiting on a porch. There is a straight road and a dirt field, a mailbox waiting for its delivery. There is a family under the trees and the swirling leaves of autumn and I see the painting so clearly I disappear into it.

Family

———— ∞ ————

Zoë fractures her wrist. She was jumping off the slide in the playground in front of our building and landed funny. I drive her up to New York-Presbyterian, to the same X-ray room in fact where we had been a few weeks ago. The technician recognizes us, giving me a didn't-we-just-see-you? look. He gives Zoë a soft cast. I find the whole thing sort of humorous.

Elise cares, I do not. Zoë's wrist is fixable. I want more broken wrists for her, more bruises, all the childhood scraped knees. There are some wounds I don't want her to experience, like being hurt by friends or by an unrequited crush, but even those I welcome. I think of eighth-grade heartache and I think, *Give her that. Guarantee that.* Broken hearts, broken legs—those are nothing. Those don't matter at all.

Elise feels that Zoë's broken wrist, on top of everything, is unfair. And it is true that Elise and I are both sad that Zoë's cast means she will not be able to swim for at least a month. It's summer, and we are going to the beach.

My family owns a beach house in Connecticut, on a hedged peninsula called Black Point that pushes into Long Island Sound. Early on Saturday morning we pile into our station wagon and drive there, stopping first at my parents' farm outside New Haven to raid their garden.

As we drive up the Merritt Parkway, I tell stories to the girls about growing up on the farm in Bethany. How I milked my goats every morning before school (and had goat milk on my cereal), how I rode my pony bareback, how my brother would pin me down and spit on me and did this until the day I chased him around the barn with a pitchfork, stories that show that our farm wasn't a typical farm.

We exit the Merritt and drive past a working dairy farm, past a blue necklace of reservoirs, then up a hill through a subdivision and there's my parents' mailbox. A hayfield tumbles into an apple orchard, and Zoë and Mia jump out of the car and run to find the dogs, passing my father as he walks up the dirt driveway. My father has curly tufts of gray hair over his ears, a dimpled smile, and when he sees us he waves both his arms. He's wearing patched corduroys and a dress shirt with holes at the elbows, his farming clothes.

The girls find the dogs, and we find my mother in the garden, her whitening hair tangled, her forehead smeared with dirt. My parents met in New Haven in the 1960s when my mother was the first woman at the Yale School of Forestry. My father asked her out to this land on their first date, and she stayed, and they built a house at the edge of the orchard and raised my brother and me. My mother is fiercely protective (I have an early memory of her throwing herself between me and a runaway horse) and wildly generous. She's picking lettuce today. She hands us baskets and orders us to take as much as we can carry.

Sometimes I tell friends I grew up in the hardscrabble heartland of the Connecticut farm belt. This is a joke. But writers and politicians often feel a need to establish their credibility, their blue-collar Americanness, by highlighting their working-class roots, preferably in Peoria. Creating a backstory of ordinariness for themselves even if they attended Wesleyan or Brown.

I cannot say that. Because growing up on this land, with my family's history, has given me every advantage. In my fourth-grade textbook there was a map of New Haven from its founding in 1638; in the bottom right corner of the New Haven Green was a small script *Cooper*. John Cooper was a prosperous farmer, and his descendents were prosperous farmers until they became prosperous lawyers, and for generations the Coopers have been practicing the family trade and my father's patched farming clothes can't hide that he's a lawyer, too. All these Coopers have been going to Yale. Another line I tell friends is that I had to go to the local college.

When my father was a student at the Yale Law School he bought this land with his professor, Guido Calabresi.

Guido lives in the original farmhouse down the hill. When Guido became dean of the law school, and I was applying to Yale, he wrote me a recommendation. When I consider this now I think it would have been hard for me not to get into Yale.

Our family's privilege comes, I hope, with responsibility. For my father I think this means protecting land. He's an environmental lawyer and has headed the Connecticut Nature Conservancy; he recently prevented a golf course development by George W. Bush's college roommate. His owly smile is a cover.

When I was growing up I found my privileged New England ancestors a little embarrassing, while my Hungarian and Jewish ancestors were mysterious and awesome. It took longer for me to appreciate the New Englanders, their thriftiness and generosity, with money or vegetables. But the wealth is always there. Our family will never have to worry about paying for a treatment.

After filling our baskets with half the garden, we pry Zoë and Mia off the dogs, then off the swing under the apple tree, and say good-bye. My parents wave from the driveway, holding the dogs' paws and making them wave, too, and we drive through Woodbridge past the compound where my grandparents lived. In the shadow of maple trees stands a large white brick house, built by my grandfather during the Great Depression. At one end of the house is a greenhouse, at the other end, up a path under the maple trees, a small writing house. It's hard to see, so we stop so I can point it out to Zoë and Mia. Dark green clapboard sides, white trim, paned windows, a chimney from a wood-burning stove poking through a shingled roof. There used to be a desk against the window at which my grandmother wrote fiction pieces for *The New Yorker* and ten novels. I'm not sure how the people who live here use it now; it's the perfect writing house. I've talked with my brother about coming here in the night and lifting it off its foundation and stealing it away on one of his flatbed trucks.

My grandmother wrote letters to her editor, the novelist William Maxwell, and sometimes Maxwell took the train to Woodbridge to edit her pieces in person, visits that were the basis for a story he wrote called "The Patterns of Love." It's about my aunt, and a missing duck. The cherubic four-year-old racing around and pestering the narrator is my father. The family that Maxwell described sounds idyllic.

When I was a senior in college I wrote to Maxwell, and through him got an interview at *The New Yorker,* and then a job there as a messenger. When I was supposed to be delivering manuscripts around the city, I'd drop in on him at his book-packed apartment on the Upper East Side and have tea. He'd give me advice, and he wrote me letters on a typewriter with a broken *e*. He was elegant and kind and reminded me of my grandfather.

Da sang in the Whiffenpoofs at Yale, was a spirited piano player at New Year's Eve parties, and took me fly-fishing. Da loved to garden, knees splayed to the side, and I remember him saying from that bent position, "Money means nothing to Da." He knew he was being funny, and knew this wasn't true, but he was also saying that other things were more important, like education or travel or health.

Da did something else. He gave me money: ten thousand dollars a year in blue-chip stocks from when I was born to the year he died, the year I went to college. That money was indispensable. It let me quit *The New Yorker,* or even work there in the first place, because few college graduates can work for eighteen thousand dollars a year in New York without help. Since quitting I have written twenty books, but that initial money was like the best grant ever. It allowed me to do what I love. Children's book authors don't earn much; I make thirty thousand dollars a book. I owe my career to my grandfather.

Or, to Elise. As we drive south we pass the Yale athletic fields, and the soccer stadium where I first saw her. She was an All-Ivy midfielder, and as I watched her with the ball at her feet, spinning around defenders and making them grasp at air, I was mesmerized. Then we started talking in the training room while getting our ankles taped and I asked her out. Elise grew up in Wisconsin, a star at Madison West High and on the regional United States junior national team. Midwestern and middle-class, she hadn't been to New Haven until her recruiting trip. Proudly Italian (mother's family from Sicily, father's from Naples), the dissimilarity between her upbringing and mine was appealing. She was also incredibly cute—small body, big personality, with corkscrew auburn hair and bright blue eyes. Though her most compelling feature may have been that she saw something in me. When we met I think we both sensed we had found each other. We fit each other, and over the years she became my family.

As we drive now through Yale's neo-Gothic campus, Elise and I sit in the front seats, pointing out to Zoë and Mia the dorm rooms where we slept, the dining halls where we ate. Libraries where Elise studied and I rarely did (I often drew students who were studying, or tried to convince friends to go outside and throw a ball). Elise's academic seriousness allowed her to graduate with honors, work as a researcher for the company that makes *Sesame Street,* then go to grad school at Berkeley. Her persistence led to a Chicago postdoc and a professorship at NYU, which in turn has given our family housing and health care, and me the freedom of being an academic spouse.

We drive out of New Haven and head east on the interstate. I put on the movie *My Neighbor Totoro* for the girls; squeaks and giggles from various creatures bubble up from the backseat. Zoë is a child who always has one ear tuned to adult conversations, so as I tell Elise about the family that married into the Coopers, someone else is listening. The Waynes were southerners and the patriarch, James Moore Wayne, a justice on the Supreme Court in the Dred Scott case, which said blacks were not citizens. His upholstered Supreme Court chair was handed down to our family, and my cat gave birth on it, her placenta making a stain that never came out.

From the back Zoë says, "The cat did *what?*"

Zoë goes back to half watching *Totoro* and I tell Elise about Justice Wayne's son, a general so useless he wasn't allowed to fight and was instead put in charge of Savannah's defenses. He pointed the guns to sea and when Sherman marched in from the land Savannah surrendered without a fight. The family story is that Savannah owes its beauty to our ancestor's incompetence. The same man also tried to introduce camels to Texas by importing a shipload of them from Egypt. Texas owes its camellessness to our ancestor. His son, maybe sensing something about his family, fled north and fought with the Union army at Antietam and Gettysburg under an assumed name, and after the war his family married into the Coopers.

The highway winds through New England and we cross the Connecticut River at Old Saybrook, the blue of the water cut by the white triangles of sailboats. Another family that married into the Coopers was the Fields, whose ancestors were sea captains who ran clipper ships from New Haven to China (their cargo was tea, and light, so they used china plates for ballast, including the blue ones we eat from each night). On a return trip one captain stopped in Hawai'i and helped King Kamehameha ferry troops to put down a revolt in Molokai. Another captain was captured by pirates off the coast of Spain and made to walk the plank.

"Did he live?" Mia says, giggling.

I am out of stories now and we exit the highway. As we slow through the town of East Lyme we roll down the windows. The air takes on a marshy heat, and we round a turn and are met by reeds and wetlands and osprey nests and a widening sky, and just before we hit the Sound there's a dirt driveway, and we downshift up through a field and there's our cottage.

Gray shingled and white shuttered, the cottage has that particular New England dilapidation that is often a cover for affluence. The house was built by my great-grandfather in 1913 and it looks it. Zoë and Mia race around under the large spruce tree that shades the cottage as Elise and I clang about inside and open windows to let in the air. The cottage is cool, with different weather in the kitchen, the pantry, the porch. There's always a breeze on this hill, which is why the local Nehantic Indians camped here. With the marsh and ocean so close it must have been like camping in the fish section of a grocery store.

We change into swimsuits and walk through the field, scattering rabbits as we go, past white gates and gray bathhouses down to the beach (the community of Old Black Point is insular and we are often confronted and asked if we're members). The beach is pretty, a pebbled turn with dunes and plum bushes and a rocky point at the far end. A wooden pier juts out through waves that are the perfect size for small children.

But with her cast, Zoë can't swim. So we stay in the sand and she and Mia build forts out of driftwood. Elise goes for a run, then walks with the girls along the water's edge as they scour for sea glass. I lie to the side, half listening to the screech of gulls and the slap of water against the underside of motorboats, glancing up from a book to watch my daughters, and I think about stories.

The stories I tell my children are only partly true. Or, at least, they have been passed down in such a way that they have become legend. Details omitted, facts scrubbed. I know that the Cooper who helped found New Haven once whipped a girl who burned down his barn and made her wear a leather halter in public. That the sea captains clubbed seals in the Pacific, trading their pelts for tea. That the captain who walked the plank was actually shot because he refused to walk the plank. I'm not sure what to think about the ancestor who thought he could introduce camels to Texas.

I know that when I tell these stories I am trying to give my daughters a sense of their history. To know that our family has been incredibly fortunate. I also hope that they appreciate this privilege but wear it lightly, and do good work. I want them to know about the repugnant Supreme Court justice but also what my cat did to his chair.

Zoë's cast comes off later in the summer and we drive to Black Point again. We walk down the beach to the rock point at the far end. The girls clamber among the rocks as they investigate tidal pools where hermit crabs scuttle and hide. Zoë has turned six, her body strong and lean in her dark blue bathing suit, her skin the color of a brown egg. Mia follows behind her sister in a pink bathing suit, her hair in bouncing pigtails, her shadow darting in and out of her sister's. Together they look like Satsuki and Mei, the sisters in *My Neighbor Totoro*. Together they are sprites.

On the other side of the rocks is a ledge over a channel. Elise leads the girls up there and they jump one after the other into the churning water below. My ankle has been hurting—a pain that is disconcerting and sharp—so I stay on the rocks.

As I watch my daughters swim, I think more about stories. Because as much as I hope they will understand the responsibility that comes with privilege, in the end that does not matter. It's the tribalism of any parent. All these stories, all the education and connections and money they represent, I give completely. No questions asked. All that has been given to me I give to them. Fair or not, I put them first. I will give them everything.

Back in the city after a weekend at the beach, I bring Zoë to Yankee Stadium. Ever since moving to New York, she has asked to see a game at the old stadium before it's torn down. So we take the subway up to the Bronx and make our way to the ticket booth. It's a Tuesday afternoon, a day game against Minneapolis, so buying two tickets in the grandstand should be easy. But the man in the booth says the only seats remaining are behind the Yankee dugout, and three hundred dollars each. I take Zoë's hand and walk to the side and crouch down next to her, explaining how we will try to scalp tickets but that today may not be our day.

As I'm talking with her I hear tapping, knuckles on glass. It's the ticket seller, beckoning me to him. I walk up and he slides me two tickets and says, "Take them. *Go.*" He motions for me to leave. So we do, though not before I ask him his name so I can write to him later and thank him.

We push through the turnstiles into the house of Ruth and Gehrig, of Mantle and Jeter. And I know, as I pick up Zoë and lift her above the jostling crowd and we walk up the ramp to our seats—the vastness of the stadium opening above us in a limitless expanse of blue stands and green grass—that I am *so* lucky. That *we* are lucky. That stories, like this one, keep giving to me, and that my family keeps giving to me, and that except for having a child with cancer, I am the luckiest man in the world.

Waiting

———— ✑ ————

It's dark in the ultrasound room, and very quiet. The room is square and plain; a framed painting of a fish and a cat hang on the walls. The curtains are drawn shut. The brightest thing in the room may be the light reflected in the glasses of the ultrasound technician as he looks into the screen of his monitor. The technician is from India or Pakistan, I'm not sure which. He tells me though, letting me know he was a respected doctor there and now has to perform rudimentary ultrasounds here in America. But I am not listening.

Zoë is lying on a gurney in a white cotton gown. I am sitting at her side, my hands folded. The ultrasound monitor is above me but I am trying not to look at it, rows of unknowable white numbers glowing on a black screen, pulsing phantoms of green and red showing my daughter's internal organs. The technician adds gel to his wand and moves it over Zoë's midsection—he is checking to make sure there are no growths or dark masses—

then punches a number into his keyboard and moves on. *Click.* He says something. I say something.

He looks closer. Measures.

Click. Click.

He moves the wand to another organ, pushing it into Zoë's belly and turning his wrist like he's carving a bowl.

Click.

Sometimes he pauses and stares. Then he stops, leans forward with one long finger and points and says, "There is the tumor."

I don't breathe. I stop breathing. I have to actually make myself breathe. My heart. I think I may be hyperventilating. The quiet is crushing. I take Zoë's hand.

I say. I start to say. The *tumor?*

"What did you . . . ?"

But I cannot finish the sentence and I feel as if the whole world has opened up beneath me but I am not falling and I am suspended and life is suspended and it is dark.

I try to concentrate on Zoë's face.

Am I mistaken? Did he say "tumor" or something else? Did he say "was" or "is"? Could this be his accent, or my hearing? I think I misheard him.

Click.

Each second is two seconds. Minutes stretch, tighten, stretch. I have never fainted before but I think I may faint.

Zoë's face is calm, and so beautiful. I keep my eyes on her face. I hear a voice from a distance, my own voice.

"How are you doing. Okay?"

I squeeze her hand.

I must be mistaken. I must be.

Now we are done. I thank the technician. I am incapable of asking him what he said. The man's face is studiously blank. I try to read his face. He knows the results, he has seen what he has seen—a new tumor, or not—but he is not supposed to tell me. But *did* he tell me?

I repack our bag with books and balls and peanut butter and jelly sandwiches, and we walk out of the hospital into yet another bright fall day. It is unbearably clear outside. We walk west on 168th Street—the blue band of the Hudson gleaming across from us, the Palisades rising in autumnal oranges and yellows—then up Fort Washington Avenue, past the security guard, and up the elevator to the pediatric oncology clinic, where we check in with the receptionists and their fixed smiles.

Dr. Lee is with another patient.

So we sit against the wall and eat our lunch, and we wait. We will meet Dr. Lee when she is done. She will tell us the results then. She will read the results once they are sent to her by the radiology department. The results are in her in-box, or they are digitally crossing Fort Washington Avenue. Out there, somewhere.

I hear the sound of heels down the hall and Dr. Lee comes into view wearing one of her soft sweaters, talking with the other family. She peels away to give Zoë a hug.

She has seen the results, or not.

"Be with you soon, okay?"

We wait.

To pass the time, Zoë and I bounce a ball between us. Then we play an invented game, hopping among the stenciled patterns on the floor, from snake to frog to lily pad. As we wait, in the stillness of the hallway, I have the same feeling I had before playing football games in college.

There was a particular almost-quiet in the locker room. The *click-clack* of shoulder pads being fastened, the soft crunch of cleats on the hard floor. No one said much. There was little eye contact. Our fullback threw up before every game and sometimes we could hear his retching from the bathroom, the gurgling of water flushing through the pipes, but otherwise a blanket of quiet settled over us. Large men waiting in silence.

I wasn't a starter and didn't play much. So for me there was the added quiet wait on the sidelines. The Yale Bowl could be roaring and the band booming with tubas, but I remained inside my quiet. A heavy quiet, where I waited behind the offensive coordinator and worried I would mess up when I eventually entered the game. When I did play, on third-down pass plays, or late in the game, another type of quiet took over. The crowd could be thirty thousand people but I was released into a stillness where it was just the grass field and the opponent in front of me, and I was able to run.

When I tell editors in the largely female world of children's book publishing that I played football at Yale it usually gets a laugh. An amused *Really?* As if I played cricket at Cambridge, or badminton for the Lycée Français. But our team was good. Our quarterback played for the Oakland Raiders after graduating (though he wasn't the smartest guy and couldn't throw a spiral and was busted in the BALCO steroid scandal). When I held hands in the huddle with our linemen—arms reaching up to young men twice my size—I was holding hands with All-Americans from Ohio and Texas and Illinois. The coaches at Yale were just as loud and stunted as at any big-time college football program.

When I tell these editors I played football at Yale I suppose I play along with the joke, adding the deprecating line that I was the weakest guy on the team. Which is true; the kicker was stronger than me. Even now I am small, and shaped like a pear. I have chubby cheeks and sloped shoulders. I don't look like an athlete.

But jokes often are not entirely jokes. Because, even at Yale, few players were as fast as I was. My legs were unnaturally large; I still have odd extra muscles in my calves. Though I was surrounded by All-Americans, in scrimmages none of them could cover me. I didn't drop the ball. I was relentless. I was the guy running extra sprints after practice.

After college I picked up a new sport, ultimate Frisbee. I shed my adolescent nerves and replaced them with the cockiness of a guy in his twenties, adding a certain football nastiness. In my first year playing in New York,

I cracked heads with an opponent, accompanied him in a bloody ambulance ride to the hospital, got stitched up, and went back to the game.

When we moved to California I joined a club team, playing against the best teams in the country. Though the competition wasn't as challenging as college football, I found I could run past people, run around them, just keep running. The more I played, the more I was able to take over games. I ran all over the field, catching throw after throw, and sometimes, inside my running, I would hear a voice.

I remember one game in Santa Cruz when a teammate threw the disc deep, beyond everyone it seemed, and it was hanging out in the blue over the Pacific Ocean and the voice said—it was both my voice and something so deep inside me I felt I was hearing it—*I am going to catch that.* So I started sprinting from midfield, legs churning as I left my defender behind, and the disc was hovering in the distance and as I got closer I could see its individual rotations and could sense the fans tensing around the field (not many fans, this was still ultimate Frisbee), and then I was diving in full horizontal at the edge of the grass, coming up with a roar, the disc in my hand.

In that moment I didn't just think I would make the play, I knew it. There was no doubt. This was arrogance, of course, but that was the point. There were probably four other guys on the field at any given time with a voice telling them they would make a play too, so playing became a competition between these interior voices. Whose silent voice was louder.

In my thirties my throwing improved and I started handling the disc, becoming both a thrower and a receiver. We moved to Chicago and I joined a team of men who had been national finalists, men who had families and didn't play in tournaments anymore but were still extremely good. If anything I played quieter now, as if I were having a conversation with myself.

Playing became dialogue: *I will run here, I will throw the disc there, we will score over there.* I found I could move other players around the field, teammates and opponents both. I could see meaning in the choreography of moving bodies, in open spaces and flying objects, sense a play before it happened and picture the arrangement of the field three seconds in the future, then run to the right place before anyone else.

The more I played, the slower the game became. I played a little removed, a little vacant. Players talk about flow, or being in the zone (and when players on the same team play this way together it is chemistry). For me it was a story. Not just one play, but a series of plays. Forgetting a bad play, imagining a better one. A game became a short story written with sweat. One in which I could beat ambiguity, defeat doubt. Legs feed the head, and I knew if my legs were right, and my head was right, we would win. I could bend narrative.

I still play ultimate, a casual game in Central Park with

friends I played with when we first lived in New York. I don't have to think much to score or make our team win. I play football only once a year, at the Yale-Harvard alumni game.

The alumni game is a tradition played the night before the actual game. It's supposed to be a friendly game of two-hand touch. The players wear their old jerseys and complain about being out of shape (someone invariably pulls a hamstring on the first play). But every year, toward the end of the game, a nose is bloodied, words are spoken, and there are flashes of the players these men used to be, even if now they are doctors or bankers.

For the past few years I have been the Yale quarterback at the alumni game, and when I drove to Cambridge this fall I hoped I would be throwing to Rich Diana. When I was growing up, Rich Diana was my hero. A powerful and muscular runner, and deceptively quick, Diana broke every rushing record at Yale. I watched him at the Yale Bowl when I went to games with my father and watched him on television in Super Bowl XVII when he played for the Miami Dolphins. He's an orthopedic surgeon in Connecticut now but seems to have maintained his old physique and skills, so I felt good when I saw him on the sidelines of Harvard Stadium slipping out of dress clothes and pulling on his blue number 33 jersey.

Harvard Stadium was empty and echoey; the only people here besides the players were workers painting a *Y* and *H* on the field. We started the game and I threw a short out pattern. Then a slant, a post, a post corner. Each play setting up the next. Creating rhythm, thinking one play ahead. Run, pass, reverse.

I had taped my ankle tight, and it held, and when defenders rushed me I ran around them. When I threw, I moved the safety with my eyes to the left and threw to the right. The game was simple, and very clear. The night took on a sort of dreamy quality as I threw one touchdown to Diana, then another. On the last play of the game we were beating Harvard by about eight touchdowns and I intercepted a last fluttery ball and ran it back the length of the field for one final score.

Afterward we showered and shared beers and I got into a long political argument with Diana, who thought Barack Obama was going to ruin the country and take away all our money. Rich Diana, my hero.

But I was willing to look past this, and I was proud of these Yale players, these All-Americans whom I had played with or grown up watching play. As I drove back to New York with my ankle wrapped in ice, I rode this feeling of pride, this endorphin rush of strength and power. And I replayed that last moment where I picked the ball out of the night sky and raced the other way, the stands a blur as my legs drove me down the field and nothing and nobody could stop me.

. . .

In the halls of the pediatric oncology clinic, we are still waiting. Zoë and I have finished our game of hopping between lily pads. We are sitting against the wall and reading books when we hear heels coming down the hallway. Dr. Lee rounds the corner and she is alone now. It's our turn. She gives us big smiles (though the thing is, Dr. Lee smiles at everyone). I stand, fumbling with my bag of books and balls as Zoë and Dr. Lee start walking ahead of me, happily talking with each other.

"So, what's new?" Dr. Lee says to Zoë. She's so good with Zoë. She is *so* good with Zoë. She asks questions and gives Zoë time to answer and they walk side by side like the oldest of friends. Diagonal friends, one tall, one short.

Dr. Lee does not say anything to me.

She has seen the results. She knows now.

As I struggle to catch up with the two of them, my mind stuck in the ultrasound room from two hours ago and careering among unfathomables, I wonder if strength means nothing. At least, my strength means nothing. Speed and power, persistence and hustle. All those muscles that have driven me over countless fields. All that confidence, all that control. All that, nothing.

We turn a corner and enter Dr. Lee's office.

Could it be there are other types of strength I lack? A softer strength, a strength of resilience, or of patience. Strength that the females in my life seem to have. Strength that would let me bend to this. Bear this.

Mine is a brittle strength. Arrogant, hard. Irrelevant. Because when faced with this moment, in this small room in this large hospital, with what feels like the life of my child hovering out in front of me, I am broken.

Dr. Lee shuts the door behind us. Zoë clambers up on the examining table. They are talking about what's new in school but I cannot speak and I am just standing.

Dr. Lee looks in Zoë's ear and asks her what she'll find in there—*Is she forgetting to tell me the results? Is she waiting to tell me when we are alone?*—and uncurls the stethoscope from her neck and starts palpating Zoë's belly and listening to her heart—*My God, Dr. Lee, please*—and it is only then, as the room starts to spin and the world begins to race headlong into a quiet that is deafening, that Dr. Lee turns and makes eye contact with me and silently mouths the words *All clear.*

And my legs, as I take my seat, buckle.

Words

A snowstorm has crept into New York, stealing across the Hudson and up the avenues and down through the streets of the Village, drifting over sidewalks and turning parked cars into hulking white beasts, insinuating itself into every crevice and bringing the city to a halt. School has been canceled. Elise has gone to her office and Zoë and Mia are home with me today. I'm at my desk writing e-mails, looking up occasionally at the snow gusting outside the window. The girls are in the hallway kicking a soccer ball. I can hear the muffled thump of the ball against a wall and then I hear yelling. A man's voice.

"No balls in the hall!"

Then louder. "NO. BALLS. IN THE HALL!"

I walk to the door. Zoë and Mia are skulking back toward me with the ball under Zoë's arm. At the far end of the hall I see one of our old neighbors halfway out his door, his bony arm pointing up at us. For my benefit he shouts one more time—"NO BALLS IN THE HALL!"— then slams his door.

I tell the girls to go inside.

I walk down the hall—our hallway is the length of a small city block—and knock at the man's door. He opens it a crack and glares out. I apologize for our disturbing him, explain that it's a snow day, that the girls are home from school, and ask if he would mind if they played at our end of the . . .

"It is *the rule*. No balls in the hall!" he interrupts and slams the door.

I knock again, louder this time.

"Okay," I say, waving my arm, "*that* end of the hallway will be for children playing." Then I swing my arm to where we are facing each other. "And *this* end of the hallway will be for old men yelling." It's not often that the words I want have found their way out of my mouth, and with that I should have walked away. However, I take one step closer and add something. "But if you *ever* yell at my daughters again," I say, *"I will kill you."*

He closes the door. I walk back down the hall. I sit at my desk.

I have been thinking about anger recently. When my friends and I get together we often share stories about anger (which we tell when the women in our lives are not around). One of our favorite stories comes from my friend Paul, and it's actually not about him, but about his father.

Paul's father was a football player, a good one. He was the quarterback at UCLA and won the Heisman Trophy.

After a few years of pro ball he retired and moved his family to Chicago. One day he was throwing a baseball with Paul on their lawn. Neighborhood kids were playing in the street. They heard a rumble, and a Pontiac Firebird roared into view and scattered the kids. A minute passed. Then, since the street was a cul-de-sac, another rumble as the Firebird came back. Paul had been holding the baseball but his father took it and threw it at the speeding car, denting in the door. The Firebird stopped. A teenager jumped out, and Paul's father—a large man a few years removed from being voted the best college football player in the country—was in the street and had the teenager backed up against the car. "If you ever speed here again," he said, "I'm not throwing a baseball, I'm throwing a shovel."

The teenager drove off. Paul resumed playing catch with his father. After a minute, Paul, who is a journalist now, asked, "Why did you say 'shovel'?" and his father said, "It's the only word I could think of."

Paul has told us this story many times. We like it because it's funny; we also empathize with his father's inability, in the heat of the moment, to make his words come out right. I've come to think of this inability as "throwing the shovel."

One of my first shovel-throwing experiences was after we moved to Berkeley for Elise's grad school. We were in Oakland at the Home Depot to buy plywood for my desk. Elise was down the lumber aisle so I didn't see or hear the man rub against her and say, "*Ooo,* feels good." But when she told me I found myself almost on top of him. I think I yelled, "Fuck you, fat boy! Fuck you, you fat boy fuck!" despite the fact that the boy was a fifty-year-old man with a bushy gray beard. He was chubby—maybe that's what I was seizing on—but I was aware in that moment of vision-narrowing anger that I could not form a sentence. I was also aware that I was now surrounded by the man's work crew—the boy was a contractor— muscled Irishmen in dirty T-shirts who said they'd beat me and leave me bloody and be on the first flight back to Dublin if I didn't stop yelling. I stopped yelling.

As we drove home that day, with plywood in the back-seat and Elise in the front and not happy with me, I pin-balled inside that *mot d'escalier* moment. What should I have said?

In my various confrontations over the years—the law-yer in Chicago, the woman in the laundry room—there seems to be a pattern. I overreact and do something wrong, then say something worse, then regret every-thing.

I think of the man at the camp in Maine who offered to kill the dog that bit Zoë. He said, "You know, I could kill that dog for you." I admired his straightforwardness, his peculiar Maine kindness. His *mot d'escalier* was a gun or an ax. Of course, it wasn't his daughter who was bit-ten, and he had the benefit of speaking after the fact, but I wanted his cool demeanor. I wish I were grounded when

I got angry. Instead I explode, then wish I could change what I said. Words fail me. Or I fail words.

The failure of language seems inextricable with cancer. Start with the word itself. "Cancer." A word that halts conversation and makes the heart skip. A word only recently not synonymous with death. A word that can change atmosphere.

Given the power of the word, it makes sense that we use other words to fight it. Words, in fact, like "fight." But fighting words seem strange. Because what if you don't like fighting? What if you fight and you lose? How do you battle something that's invisible? Can cancer be an enemy if it's inside us? Who is fighting whom? How do you fight for someone else? And why use fighting words at all when they have nothing to do with the rampant multiplication of cells, the chemical and biological minutiae of treatment. Cancer is just a physical fact, an unasked-for visitor in the night, and whether we fight or not is immaterial to the fact that it is here.

I blame the Republican political consultant Frank Luntz for this rhetorical strangeness. Luntz coined the term "death tax" for taxing wealthy peoples' inheritance and "energy exploration" for oil drilling. He saw that manipulating the words around an issue changed the issue itself. This was cynical stuff. Add words like "freedom" or "America," and maybe the image of a blond child, and the argument was won. Facts didn't matter, the phrasing did.

But we communicate in phrases all the time: "To be

honest with you." "This is the life." "That'll be the death of me." This is why I dislike parties where conversations can become a numbing series of phrases. Or why I avoid small talk in elevators, which is invariably about the weather (being stuck in an elevator with Frank Luntz on the way to a party is my idea of hell). So while fighting words make sense to encourage cancer research, to show we are doing *something,* the combative imagery doesn't feel right.

I do not believe, with cancer, that metaphors work. Cancer is not comparable. Cancer is not *like* this, *as if* that. There are no words that could adequately describe the worry felt for a loved one. Metaphors elude us. Is cancer really "a climb up a mountain with false summits" or "an unasked-for visitor in the night"?

As a children's book writer I find this maddening. Children's books should be about making a few words count. Spare sentences, clear metaphors. Of course, complete clarity is impossible (an impossibility from which no words, these or any other, are exempt). We want words to be clear, yet how can they be when life is not?

I wonder if this is why we get upset. We can't find the right words, and that makes us angry. Then we say the wrong words, and that makes us angrier. Then we regret our words and cycle downward, throwing shovels the whole time.

At some point, when my frustration with language

threatens to overwhelm me, I return to single words. Not "fight" or "battle," but words that feel more honest to me, like "kind" or "care." Or I turn to something even smaller, because with my daughter it comes down to one letter: *s* or *d*. "Has" or "had." A sneaky *s,* a definitive *d,* and the difference between those two letters is as wide as the world (simile).

This winter I have been editing my children's book on farms. Through icy sleet I biked over the Brooklyn Bridge and up slushy Park Slope, then beneath the whitened trees of Prospect Park to the designer's apartment in Flatbush. As I shed my wet jacket, and borrowed warm socks, the designer made us tea and we sat at her desk clutching mugs, staring into her computer screen.

When I worked at *The New Yorker* I helped out in the art department. The designer was French-Canadian and as we looked over page proofs of the magazine she would murmur in her lilting accent, "Love, love, love." I mention this to the book designer and soon we are both murmuring, "Love, love, love," too. One word, repeated, as we passed the cursor over the images—widening a field, reducing the size of a barn, moving a rooster to the left, shaking our heads when something didn't look right. As our eyes passed back and forth, I began to think of editing as weeding. Weeding out a word or an animal, unearthing a cleaner page by making more white space. There was only one word we added and it was not "love," or "rooster." It was "and."

"And" is my new favorite word. There's something about it. A pause, a breath before the end, a last chance to say something. It says, *Listen, I am about to bring this piece home.* A wheelhouse word used in the final sentences and paragraphs of too many books to mention. "And one fine morning—" on the last page of *The Great Gatsby.*

"And" is the writer's prayer: *I have tried to communicate with you. I am not sure if I have succeeded, but please, try to understand me. Give me one last word. And.*

It is still snowing outside. I am still at my desk. I have written a letter to the old man down the hall in which I have apologized for saying the awful thing I said. I do not mention anything about having a child with cancer, because that is no excuse. I don't mention that it has been one year since the end of my daughter's treatment. I don't say that we went to the hospital last week for her scans and that they were clear. I do not mention that her cancer has made me angry and protective and wild.

I print out the letter and take a pencil to it. I check the spelling, the grammar. I make the letter tighter and print it a second time. Then I seal it in an envelope and walk down the hall.

As I slip the envelope under the man's door, I am

aware that our words never reach our intended audience in the way we would like, but I think that our attempt at connection—that our words say what we want them to—may be the most human of all hopes.

Later I find out that I slipped the letter under the wrong door.

Table

————— ✀ —————

I have three goals for my thirties. The first is to win the Pulitzer Prize, the second is to be on *Fresh Air* with Terry Gross, the third is to build a wooden kitchen table. I have decided to concentrate on the table.

Over the holidays we drive to Massachusetts to the small town in the forested middle of the state where my brother lives on a farm with his family. Their farmhouse is a white wooden Cape Cod built in 1760, with a mudroom off the back and a low red barn off the mudroom, which my brother has turned into a wood shop.

In the spring and summer my brother builds cross-country jumps for equestrian three-day eventing, massive structures he carves out of tree trunks with his chain saw. Last fall, he designed and built a barn for his farm. In the winter, to keep his hands busy, he goes out to the wood shop and plays with wood. He has a lathe, a planer, about five circular saws of various degrees of danger, all of which will help build my table.

So while our wives take care of the children (when we visit his farm we revert to gender roles from the 1760s), my brother and I retreat to the wood shop. We pick boards of cherry milled from the local sawmill and feed them into the whirring planer. My brother is not very talkative and directs me with juts of his chin. I start working an orbital sander as he frowns at the wood. He barely uses tools to measure, feeling his way into the table as he lays out skirts and legs, tongues and grooves.

We come late to lunch, our curly hair flecked with sawdust. Then back to the wood shop with mugs of coffee. We build through dusk and into the night, the wood shop a flurry of machinery and concentration. At midnight Elise brings us slices of chocolate cake and cans of Coke. We eat and keep working. Sometimes I stop and just watch my brother. My brother is an artist with wood. I am not, so I keep working the sander, trying my best to make everything smooth.

The table is standing now in the center of our apartment in New York. Sturdy and strong legged, the few nicks and marks have only added to its beauty. As I lean against it and pass my hands over it, my eyes watering as they get lost in its rings and knots, I think this table may be the most beautiful thing I have ever made (watched someone else make), so beautiful it feels symbolic of something larger.

. . .

My view of the table is a little different when it first comes into our apartment. Because I am lying on our couch and looking up at it, my leg in a cast. A few weeks after the Yale-Harvard alumni football game I went to a doctor, and he looked at X-rays of my foot and shook his head and said I had the ankles of an arthritic eighty-year-old. So after our visit to my brother's farm I have surgery.

In the days following the operation I hop around our apartment, or ask Zoë and Mia to bring me glasses of water or the newspaper as I lie on the couch. When we "walk" to school, my crutches allow me to vault over those maddening ice puddles at the intersection of sidewalk and street, the ones that make New Yorkers mutter *Fuck!* This is small consolation because crutching around the city in the winter is as fun as root canal surgery.

Which is what I have a week later. I crutch to the subway, crutch to the dentist's office, hop into the chair, where the dentist proceeds to excavate the dark recesses of my mouth. Dr. Weintraub is sweet and solicitous. *Bubbe,* tell me if it hurts! *Bubbe,* we're almost done! *Bubbelooo!* As he drills he tells me his son wasn't accepted by Penn and might have to go to SUNY Purchase, or a kibbutz. I gargle sympathetic responses through blood, then crutch home.

The next day I get the flu.

That night I cannot sleep. I tumble out of bed and stagger to the couch and turn on the television. Right leg sore in its cast, left leg sore from hopping, hands calloused from crutching, teeth throbbing, head feverish, I begin watching a movie starring a perpetually shirtless and whooping Matthew McConaughey, and something about the combination of all these elements, with the addition of the whooping McConaughey, sends me into delirium. I cry out to Elise and take a cab to Times Square, home of the only clinic open at this hour. After being pumped with antibiotics I come home and collapse on the couch.

When I wake, the girls are sitting around the table, eating pancakes and looking at me with syrup-covered grins. I must look pretty pathetic.

As winter melts into spring, even as my health and ankle improve, my irritability gets worse. I'm irritated by everything. I visit schools to read my books and have no patience with the children. All of whom, like the weather, are dripping (a general rule of reading books in schools is that the child who drips the most will be the one who holds your hand). Or they are interrupting (another rule is that the child who just got a puppy will tell you about it at least four times). It makes me wonder why I write books for children. I have always felt lucky to be a children's book author but as I crutch away from these schools I do not feel it.

I have dispiriting meetings with editors. One flips

through sketches I've done for a book about a dog who sits on a porch, a look of real concern clouding her face. What is the dog's motivation? she asks. What does the dog *want*?

"He wants to lick his balls!" I say.

I do not say that. But with children's books one often ends up getting in impossible conversations about the impossible. Can the mouse read? Should the monkey wear pants? Will the dog need to pee if he sits on the porch all day? Questions like these are the reason that, for the most part, the children's books I write are nonfiction. Yet it seems everyone wants to get into children's books. Each week I receive a note from someone who wants my opinion about his idea for a book, but what he really wants is for me to set him up with my publisher. These people are often bankers who cashed out and now want to "get in touch with the creative side." But I always talk with them, because their idea could be good (it rarely is) and try to remember that people have helped me.

But with celebrities writing children's books, children's book authors are squeezed. Children's books are already the ugly stepchild of publishing, the value of our work negligible. One mother at Mia's preschool asks me to paint animals on the wall of her children's bedroom. I paint pigs and pandas, and since she is a friend of a friend, ask her to give me a few bottles of wine in return. Somehow she doesn't.

People would never take advantage of a lawyer in this way (though no lawyer would ask to be paid in wine, so maybe I'm not that professional). Another friend of a friend asks me for a painting of his wife's restaurant. He's a police officer. When I finish the painting he asks me to lower the price. It's hard to say no to a cop, though I do add some details to the painting (with my sketchy style it's not easy to make out the orgy I paint in the apartment above the restaurant). The policeman frames the painting and gives it to his wife.

Sometimes, as an artist, it's merely a matter of respect for time. As I sketch layouts at Jack's for my next book, parents from PS 41 sit down next to me. They just had a PTA meeting, or have a day off from work, and want to have fun. "This is so fun hanging out with you!" they say, assuming I'm not working. Even my café is irritating me.

At night I lie on the couch with my leg up and complain: parents, publishers, bankers, cops, everyone. As my list of irritations grows, I know something else is going on. This isn't just about work, or my ankle. My irritations are exacerbated by my worry about my daughter and her upcoming trip to the hospital. But how much, really? Wasn't it possible to have irritation independent of worry? Couldn't I be irritated just because?

In other words, could I be a New Yorker? Complaining is what New Yorkers do. We complain about our apartments, our work, the person next to us on the subway.

Our complaints often are pleasurable, like scratching a scab. So when Barney comes over and complains about Brooklyn real estate, and Elise complains about parents at Mia's preschool who obsess over lice, and I complain about my café, we are sort of enjoying ourselves.

So I'm not sure where irritations end and anxiety begins. I can't tease the two apart. I change cafés instead.

I say good-bye to Jack's, and good-bye to my crutches. I hobble in an ankle boot around the corner to Joe Coffee. Joe has the same clattering espresso machine as Jack's, but better coffee and bigger windows through which I can watch New Yorkers on their way to the subway and work, or tourists—often German gay men with complicated eyewear—taking photos of themselves in front of the GAY STREET sign out front.

I go back to laying out my children's book, a book about a beaver lost in the city, but then start overhearing the Joe regulars. Old men, always here, always loud, who sit against the walls of the café and have a way of talking past one another. At first this is interesting, then it becomes odd. One says he likes his coffee with a touch of hot water, the next says San Francisco has gotten too crowded, the third says he just installed a new faucet on his bathtub and it isn't working so good. Despite the fact that I will be an old man complaining in a café one day, I find myself working with both hands cupped over my ears. Then Malcolm Gladwell walks through the door under his unruly halo of hair and sits down next to me.

Trying to work on my book while Gladwell works on his proves impossible. Joe is finished, too.

Ever since the owner of Three Lives & Company put my paperback in his bookstore's window, he and I have become friends. Toby is tall and spectacled, with a faint sprinkling of hair, and we often get together for coffee. We talk about coffee, too, and he tells me about a café he discovered in Brooklyn. So after my ankle boot comes off I bike over the Brooklyn Bridge and down a cobblestone street to a tree-lined block near the water. I don't know the name of the café but it has wood tables and wide windows—through one of which I can watch traffic on the Brooklyn-Queens Expressway drifting slowly past.

I know no one here, no one knows me. A woman on my left reads and breast-feeds. A man on my right corrects school papers written in French. Another woman makes a business call while looking at her infant so it looks like she's giving financial advice to a baby. I enter that semidistracted space where I am able to work.

One day I look up from my sketchbook and see a man glaring back at me. On his face is a tremendous frown. It takes me longer than it should to see that the man, in the reflection of the café's window, is me. Forehead knotted, lower lip curled over itself, furiously gripping a pencil. The sad thing is, at that moment, I didn't feel irritated. I was just working. Irritation seems to be my natural state.

With this dispiriting thought I come home to paint. I cut paper and turn on music and when I am done I tape the paintings on the wall above my desk (or send ones that don't quite work to my grandmother, who just celebrated her hundredth birthday). The apartment fills with paintings of beavers and rivers and the Chicago skyline.

When Elise calls from the hospital I am painting a wooden water tower in the skyline. We talk a minute—it takes only a second to know Zoë's scans are clear—and then I put down the phone. I put down my brush and walk over to the table and rest my hands on it, staring into its cascading rings. I can see that wood is a living thing, alive and always changing, different than it was even a month ago, and as I look harder my eyes become lost in it, pooling into its lines and seams of sap, and I stand there for a long time with my hands on the table.

I'm afraid it was only much later that I realized my brother made this table for me because he knew I needed it. That he loved me, and was trying to understand. That he was speaking in the way he knew how. It struck me too—I wonder how I missed this before—that my brother is a Cooper. In other words, a woodworker.

My brother gave me an orbital sander after our visit to his farm, and a stack of cherry and maple, and sometimes when I am done painting for the day, I go out to the balcony and take the sander and turn the blocks of wood into cutting boards. Around and around, circling over something so simple my mind stops. No words, no paintings, just wood.

Maybe I am trying to smooth what is rough, ease my worry into a cut of maple. I am not sure, but I stay out here and work over this wood, this thing with no real goal. If I do have a goal—that my child continues to be well—it is one that is not up to me.

Orchard

—— ∞ ——

We are flying to Italy this summer. It will be Zoë and Mia's first big trip. We will stay in Florence, then drive south through the countryside. Elise and I are looking forward to the food, and to giving our daughters a taste of their Italian heritage. We have promised them we will eat gelato every day.

Raising children can be like a meal. As if parents were cooks, and experiences were ingredients, and there were a recipe: take two cups of friends, one bike, ten swimming lessons, a scoop of museums, a thousand books, a teaspoon of math, a pinch of Italy. Stir well. Serve to two girls.

The experience, or skill really, that I most want to give my daughters is knowing how to throw. When I was a boy I was always throwing: footballs, baseballs, snowballs, apples. Targets were trees, barns, and unfortunate cows. One of my favorite games was throwing apples at road signs from the moving passenger seat of our rusted Peugeot station wagon. My mother would drive me on country roads to Barney's house and I would hurl the apples—rotten ones were best—into SPEED LIMIT signs with a satisfying *splat*.

I mentioned this to Zoë and Mia when we were at my parents' farm in the fall, so we gathered apples and drove around. I could hear the occasional *splat* until the girls ran out of apples, then we headed back to New York and somewhere around Fairfield I looked in the rearview and saw apples bouncing down the parkway—and both girls grinning at me—and realized they had hoarded apples and had been throwing them the whole time.

I was so proud. Not only were my girls throwing, they were being a little bad. In one motion, and in two ways, they were knocking down the phrase "throw like a girl."

I can't stand the phrase "like a girl." It's a mean phrase—from "throwing" to "fighting" to "crying"—and I try to challenge it with my parenting. I've taught Zoë and Mia how to farmer-blow their noses, to burp with real power. I've taught them the rules of football at Giants games, how to break a trout's neck when fishing. I've given them Swiss Army knives and am looking forward to buying them their first BB gun.

Beyond these stereotypes, I just want my girls to be assertive. Able, really. Because the phrase "like a girl" is all about inability. A diet of don't. *Don't* sweat, *don't* swear, *don't* speak up. Prohibitions that start with girls and lead to women. When I see women apologizing before they speak, or covering their mouths as they laugh, I think these women's self-doubt would be less pronounced if they had spent more time throwing balls when they were girls, and less time on their hair.

Women are constrained by looks. Because what gender would change the color of their hair? Or alter its shape with hot irons? Or cover their faces with powder, or add fake eyelashes to their real eyelashes? Or paint their fingernails, stick hoops through their ears, or wear shoes with six-inch heels that pinch their toes?

A more telling question may be, Why does one gender watch the other gender do all this stuff to themselves? Sometimes I think history has been one big conspiracy orchestrated by men to keep women down. Men have no problem when women busy themselves with their looks because it distracts women from seeing that men control everything else.

You can't vote. Have a necklace.

Because what gender would make the other gender put fake hair over their real hair? Or force the other gender to cover their bodies in sheets? (I'd have no problem with burkas if men wore them, too.) Or cut off their genitals? Or use ancient texts to confirm their gender's authority over the other? Or not allow the other gender to drive, or pay them less for doing the same work? Basically do *anything* that treated their own daughters and mothers and sisters in any way that was anything but equal.

As a man I look at men with dismay, and at boys with

suspicion. Boys in my daughters' classes who bully class-mates, who won't pass the ball, who use the phrase "like a girl." These boys will grow up to be monsters, I am sure of it.

When I start seeing the world in such rigid and gen-dered terms, it is Elise who reels me back. Reminds me of thoughtful boys we know. Reminds me that I was a boy, and that we are raising two humans, not theories. And I know from watching Elise teach our daughters how to be inquisitive scientists, as well as letting them use her lipstick, that children have many cooks and are fed many foods.

Still, I believe that fathers of girls have particular responsibility, so when I pick Zoë and Mia up after school my bag is packed with balls. We walk west past Three Lives & Company—its awnings flapping in the breeze, its windows shining with the covers of books—and Toby sees us and comes out to say hello. As he and I talk about English Premier League football, Zoë and Mia take their soccer ball out of my bag and start kicking it against the wall. After the ball rolls into the street a third time we say good-bye and keep heading west.

Hudson River Park is a slender strip of trees that hugs Manhattan's western shoreline. Piers poke into the river at erratic intervals. On the pier across from Charles Street is a small turf field, and here we unpack and start throwing. First, football. The girls wrap their fingers around a Chicago Bears Nerf; sometimes they throw spirals. The ball is soft but after I knock Mia in the head with it we switch to baseball. With a Wiffle ball I show the girls how to throw curveballs, then I pitch and they take turns swinging their Chicago Cubs bat.

Zoë and Mia play like their personalities. Mia carefree, whipping the bat like she's whacking a piñata. Zoë persistent, refusing to stop until she consistently hits line drives. After I plunk her with a breaking ball that does not break, we switch to soccer.

With soccer I have less to teach. Zoë and Mia started playing on a team in the fall and already have the feet of their mother. Instinctive, almost casual, touching the ball as if their insteps were palms. Mia is a dribbler, Zoë prefers passing. Both have the skill of knowing where to be on the field. I, however, have the soccer skills of a football player and after kicking the ball over the pier's railing and into the river, our game is done.

Zoë and Mia glare at me, fists on hips. Once I promise to replace their ball, we walk south along the river, and just before we turn back toward home we look into the lowering sun and see a woman flying through the air.

There's a trapeze school on the roof of Pier 40. Nets and ropes, and catapulting aerialists. The girls stare up with wide eyes. It's amazing seeing them see something for the first time. Or starting something new—gymnastics for Zoë, ballet for Mia—that becomes theirs alone. All the experiences that show that despite the horizontal scar on Zoë's side, cancer has little to do with her.

For Zoë, cancer is something that happened in the past. The trips every three months to the hospital an unwelcome interruption from school. She doesn't talk about cancer, doesn't want to be different (Mia is more curious, in fact, more interested in the details of cancer and her sister). We know this may change as Zoë grows and understands more, but now we try to follow her matter-of-fact lead and make our lives as normal as we can. Sometimes we succeed.

This feels most possible when it's just me and my daughters playing alongside the river and I'm trying to shape them with varying degrees of success, and I am just their father. Where the greatest effect of cancer on my parenting may be an impatience with time. There should be no waiting. If there are experiences I want to share, I want to share them today. Throwing balls, taking trips. We must do everything *now*.

We arrive in Florence. After a nap at the apartment on the south bank of the Arno where we're staying, we walk over the bridge into the city center. Zoë and Mia skip in front of me in matching butter-colored sundresses, holding Elise's hands. We climb to the top of the Duomo, the buildings scattered beneath us in wedges of russet and peach. We eat *fagioli sgranati* at a small restaurant in Santa Croce. I pay the girls one euro to taste my *caffè crema,* which they promptly spit out.

We go to museums and they race through the galleries and point at statues of scowling men: "That one looks like Papa!" They write and draw in their journals on the shady side of piazzas, then toss coins in fountains. We eat gelato every day, as promised.

At night we sit on the roof of the apartment and watch fireworks from the festival of San Giovanni cascading above us. The next day Elise takes the girls to yet another *gelateria* and I go to the Piazza Santa Croce and watch a four-hundred-year-old game called *calcio storico*. Twenty-seven of the toughest men from each Florentine neighborhood wearing nothing but puffy Renaissance pants try to throw a ball into nets but really just stand around in the dirt of the piazza and pummel one another until blood runs down their fronts. There are no rules to *calcio storico*. The winning team gets a cow. (Sometimes I do love my own gender.)

After five days of devouring Florence we rent a car and drive into the country. We drive slowly as the roads are winding and tight, and the vineyard and cypress landscapes are curvaceous, so I am often pulling over to sketch. As I draw, the girls walk in the fields around me. Elise picks wildflowers while Zoë and Mia pick snails off the underside of leaves.

We stop at a hotel outside a town of stone towers. After unpacking—the girls bouncing back and forth between the two beds—I decide to go for a run. It's my first run since my ankle surgery and I start tentatively down a dirt path. After a mile the path rises through the gray-green trees of an olive grove, and as I run among the freckled shadows I pick up clods of dirt and throw them into the trunks of the trees with a satisfying *splat*.

This olive grove looks like the orchard where I grew up. A tree-covered hill, a view across a valley—just replace that distant Italian hill town with West Haven. When I was a boy I would come home after school and walk to our orchard with my goats so they could graze. I sat in the grass and read as the goats orbited around me—I was a planet and they were moons—and could hear their chewing as it grew louder—they were meteors!—then one of the goats would lie against my back and I would reach out and touch her.

I have always thought I knew the "right" way to touch an animal. Behind the ear, or under the ribs, so that when I see someone touching an animal "wrong" I want to guide their hands. My goats depended on me for everything from scratching to feeding to milking; only later did I see how much I depended on them.

Humans think we grow everything, but we don't think how we ourselves are grown. How we are cultivated. How dogs have thrived by making themselves indispensable, how corn has spread around the world by making itself bountiful. How this olive grove, by nurturing the humans who lived here—who in turn watered and pruned and harvested it—ensured its own existence.

Maybe this is true of children. Our love makes us care

for them, and they in turn shape us. So maybe raising children is not a meal with parents as cooks. Maybe we're all one olive grove, everyone growing everyone. I mean, somehow my daughters got me to bring them to Italy and feed them all this gelato.

I run back to the hotel. Elise and the girls have discovered the hotel pool, hidden behind a wall of cypresses. I find them at the pool's edge in white terrycloth bathrobes that reach to their feet, staring at the water.

The water is really cold. Elise is trying to convince Zoë and Mia it's not *that* cold, and after some toe dipping they toss off their bathrobes and jump, turning the pool into a riot of splashing and shrieking, before coming out and wrapping back in their robes—bodies shivering, teeth chattering—and waiting a minute before tossing off their robes and doing it again.

I take off my sneakers. I want to tell my daughters about the olive grove I found, how it reminded me of the orchard where I grew up. I would like to tell them that they give more to me than I could possibly give to them. But this can wait; they are in their game. So I sit and watch them play, as the shadows from the cypresses spread across the water in bands of dark and light, and I stay there watching for some time.

Cycling

———— ∞ ————

A feeling of inexorability enters our home the week before our next quarterly trip to the hospital. The days are unstoppable—Monday, Tuesday, Wednesday, Thursday— each one bringing us closer to Friday morning when either Elise or I will walk with Zoë over to West Fourth Street and take the subway uptown.

Elise and I are talkers. We talk with our hands, we talk in waves, our sentences overlapping. We are not a couple that shares comfortable silences. We like to gossip and argue; there are few thoughts we don't speak out loud. But this week it is possible we are more quiet with each other.

Elise has a smile bigger than she is. She has a smile that gathers people to her, but I think her smile is meant for me. When she smiled at me in college I was taken in and did everything I could to keep her smiling, and years later her smile is something I am still trying to make happen, every day. But this week it is possible that the smiles Elise and I share are fewer and tighter.

These are small changes, almost imperceptible even to ourselves. Mostly I think Elise and I have not changed with each other these last few years. It could be we have become closer, in the same way that muscles strengthen at the spot where they rip. But how could we know? We are close to each other; we were always close to each other. Elise, as a researcher, would say that there is no way to study this, no way to measure the data. Our sample size is too small.

I know that together we are strong. Dependent, standing back to back. The night before we go to the hospital we lie in bed and just before turning off the light we turn to each other and say, *Everything will be okay.*

That is when we are together.

Because I also know, as I drift into sleep, or if I wake and am lying alone with my thoughts in that seemingly endless stillness between night and dawn, I can't help thinking that maybe this time *everything will not be okay.* Or if I am walking the streets of the Village, or biking along its avenues, my mind racing off on tangents and speeding into various possibilities, then it is hard to stop myself from imagining the worst. Though, when biking, I am mostly thinking about not getting in a wreck.

I have been in three bike wrecks since we moved to New York. The first was in Central Park when a man darted in front of me to retrieve the top of his water bottle and I crashed into him. The second was on the Brooklyn Bridge when a tourist taking a photograph backed into the bike lane and I crashed into him. The third was in front of the girls' school when a cab door opened and I crashed into it, and over it.

After each wreck my bike was a little damaged. Scraped frame, snapped chain, crooked derailleur, and I had to walk to our local bike shop to replace the part. I was a little damaged, too. Bloodied knee, bruised elbow, cheese-gratered shin. I started to think of myself in the same terms as my bike. Bent but not broken.

Though even if I was not hurt, the accumulation of all the near misses on my rides around the city were leaving a mark. A visible fraying. I'd get off my bike with a pounding heart and enter some café in Brooklyn and there would be a pretty young woman looking at me.

Or not looking at me. In that moment when our eyes did not meet, when the young woman's eyes passed through me, I sensed not only how disheveled I must appear, but also that I was losing my looks.

If the woman paused to look, this is what she would see: a man approaching middle age in a faded T-shirt and worn corduroys. Unshaven face, creased eyes, thinning gray-flecked hair. Add the most important fact that I was never good-looking to begin with and it was no wonder she didn't see me.

The young woman invariably would be wearing a sweater with a pony on it. It would be spectacularly ugly, but charming on her, with her long hair falling over an exposed neck and mind-pausing breasts. Her youth and attractiveness were all that mattered.

I find I am attractive only in certain contexts, when my looks don't matter. When I sign books at schools in suburban New Jersey, or on the Upper East Side, the school mothers with their put-together clothes and held-together faces flash me gleaming white smiles. I am "the author" here; maybe my T-shirt and corduroys look a little roguish. What these mothers and I share is that neither of us look how we used to (though they do a better job of disguising this), and we know it.

As I age into invisibility, at least in the eyes of the young and attractive, there are rare occasions when a woman will notice me from across a café and do a double take. A moment of eye contact that reflects our desire to be desired. I will be sad when this no longer happens. Especially because these fleeting moments with the women of New York and their inane sweaters make me happy to come home and see Elise.

Scarf weather has come to New York. As I bike over the Brooklyn Bridge and down to Red Hook, a stiff wind blows in from the harbor and shakes the leaves on the trees, making them rattle against one another. It's the weather of premonition, weather before a storm. I ride over cobblestone streets in the lee of loading cranes and stop at a café called Fort Defiance, named after the fort where the Continental army shot off their cannons at British warships in 1776 during the Battle of Brooklyn.

As I warm myself with a coffee, I notice a man on the other side of the café. He's probably ten years older than I am. He's wearing a sports coat and black-framed glasses. He has a trim goatee. The woman across from him must be his wife. He looks up from his phone and mutters something to her; she mutters something back. They share the irritability of a couple who are too familiar with each other. They look miserable.

When I see couples like this I fill with unease. I don't want to become this man. I don't want to become a middle-aged man who grows facial hair and discovers fashion. It looks like he's fighting aging, and losing. Though the saddest part seems to be that there is no love between him and the woman he's with, a chasm of indifference.

On my bike home from Fort Defiance it starts to rain. I think more about looks and wear. We live in an it-gets-better age, but what happens when it does not? When the rips in our muscles do not get stronger, when wounds don't heal. Our bodies decay as it is, then add anxiety eroding from the inside. While the possibility that my daughter's cancer will recur becomes less with each passing scan, I don't know if my worry has lessened. In fact, I think it's grown. I live in fear of the unexpected phone call, the next trip to the hospital.

Consider having a day that asks the question, *Will your child live?* Then repeat that day every three months. How could that not damage, not wear down, not age. The answer to this is clear enough and I keep biking as the rain picks up, lashing the cobblestones.

There is a stone wall outside the front door of the hospital, and when Zoë and I come out on Friday we stop at this wall. This is where I call Elise, reaching her just before she teaches her class to tell her everything is okay. Zoë scrambles onto the wall and takes the phone to say hello as I remove the ID band from her ankle. Then I lift Zoë in my arms—increasingly harder to do, her legs bumping into mine—and we head to the subway. As we go I know I am radiant. Or, looked at another way, handsome.

We ride the subway downtown. Elise has picked up Mia from school and we meet on a corner in the Village. Elise gives me a smile (her everyday smile but I know better). She kisses Zoë as I lift Mia up and spin her around. All three are wearing their hair in braided pigtails.

Then I hug Elise. As we hold each other the decades collapse, from the time we first held each other in college, to when she was a young mother and we held a baby between us, to the parents we are now. She and I have grown up together, our temples graying in small curls from these last years, and in this moment our aging feels timeless and natural, as if we could age with grace, and everything is seamless and everything is good.

In the afternoon Elise goes for a run along the river, and when she comes home I get on my bike. I head to Brooklyn, pedaling hard up the slope of the Williamsburg Bridge. At the top of the bridge I can see wisps of fog scudding the East River below, the yellow Domino Sugar sign sliding through the pilings. I am flying up here, as if life itself has been given to me.

But there's a plummeting downside to this high, as sure as the other side of the bridge. Just this morning I took the train to the hospital in a state of dread, and now I am in a state of euphoria bordering on mania, and in three months I must travel these emotions again. Circular and grinding. A pattern I can't break.

I am a boat on these concrete waters. Tacking up avenues and crossing bridges, looking for safe harbor in some warm and lighted place. I feel young and I feel free, but I am going so fast that I don't know how to stop.

Wild

———— ∾ ————

In the rain forests of eastern Ecuador, outside the small missionary town of Archidona, a large howler monkey is about to punch my brother-in-law in the head. I am fifty feet away, rooted in place. Jeff does not see the monkey and bends to look at a tropical plant at the exact moment the monkey swings down and takes a swipe at him, missing his head by an inch and retreating into the canopy with a scream.

Jeff and his family have been living in Ecuador this year, teaching English and learning Spanish. We have flown here over the holidays, to visit them in Quito and drive around the country. It's been a great trip, until the monkey. We will be staying at this hostel in the rain forest for the next three days, surrounded by monkeys.

We cannot be here. We must leave now. The fact that this monkey—who we learn has a reputation around the hostel—could leap out at any moment and attack my daughters makes me so angry it renders me speechless. But it's not like I want to talk about it either.

At times like this it feels that my fear about cancer is in my head alone. Friends have moved on. They say, "She's cured, right?" Or they don't ask. Or, if they are literary, they suggest I read Lorrie Moore's "People Like That Are the Only People Here" (the much-admired short story about a parent and her child with cancer). But I cannot read that story, and I cannot read articles about cancer in the Science section of the *Times,* and when an ad comes on TV for a children's cancer hospital I change the channel. My inability to speak about cancer has calcified. There are times I don't think about it—a few days in Italy, a few hours when I'm playing sports. But when Zoë's scans are approaching, or when I feel threatened, the thought rarely leaves my head. My own voice, hectoring me: *My daughter had cancer, my daughter has cancer, my daughter had cancer.* Had, has. Has, had. Had.

In these moments I fold inward and no amount of love and understanding from friends or family can penetrate this little mind prison. I wrestle by myself and think about fairness.

When Zoë and Mia argue their favorite line is, "That's not fair!" A line said so frequently I have started telling them the word "fair" does not exist. Then I look it up in the dictionary and hold my thumb over the word and say, "See? No fair!"

But I think about fairness all the time.

I think of smokers who smoke despite knowing they invite cancer. Or people who go to tanning salons. Or those who have cancer and treat it with herbs. Anyone, really, who is careless with his or her life. Drunk drivers, helmetless bike messengers, idiots who opt out of vaccinations, hikers who venture into national parks without water.

Because it's not just their life. They are hurting those who love them and endangering those around them. Intentionally or not, they are also offending those who *want* life, who are clinging to existence as hard as they can. We have all been given *one life,* a miracle really, and to treat this lightly is unspeakable. Unfair. It's like splashing a glass of water on your head next to someone who is dying of thirst.

I think of the suicidal. I have no problem with offing oneself at the end of life (just make it clean and have your body delivered to the morgue). But someone whose body *works*? I think of the children in the pediatric oncology clinic at NewYork-Presbyterian, needles and tubes curving into their small bodies. *They* would like a pair of working lungs, a body that won't fail them. *They* would like life.

Cancer, it's poorly distributed.

When I fall into hyperbole like this, I start to see the entire world as unbalanced and unfair. A world where nothing makes sense and everything is horrible, where there is little difference between a tumor and an aggressive monkey. I'm dimly aware that this is illogical, that I'm not seeing clearly. Or, seeing things that aren't there.

So when Zoë and Mia are playing with their cousins next to a stream in what must be one of the most beautiful places on earth, I am watching the jungle. Vigilant, every nerve on edge, peering at shadows. My daughter looks happy and healthy (but she looked healthy the day before she was diagnosed). While it would seem to anyone else that this is a child happily dancing in an inch of water, to me it looks like she is dancing on a precipice.

After failing to fend off a monkey attack that never materializes, we fly home. A few days later I get a message from Maurice Sendak. I had sent him an advance copy of *Farm,* and he tells me to give him a call. We talk for an hour, and he swears the entire time. Damn this, damn that. He growls about publishing and the state of children's books. He invites me to visit him at his home in Connecticut. I get off the phone impressed by his irascibility.

Sendak tells me he's been reading William Blake so after we talk I look up that poem about the lamb, the only Blake poem I remember. But with my mind preoccupied with fairness, all I can think about is something else I read about lambs. How sometimes baby lambs are born and within minutes pecked to death by ravens as they struggle to stand.

Nature is brutal enough without humans. We add discrimination. Conscious thought that lets us sell humans into slavery, or put them in gas chambers. Given our capacity for awfulness, I'm amazed humans ever turn to religion. I think how Abraham placed his son Isaac on a pyre when God told him to. I know it's just a parable, but its message seems to be that we're supposed to have faith. Believe that there's a plan and that God will provide (which He does with a sacrificial ram, but pretty late in the story I think). I look at Abraham, who must be the worst father in literature, and at God, who acts here like a real jerk, and all I think is: We're supposed to have faith in *these guys*?

If I have faith at all it is in science. Faith in medicine, faith in the CT scan machine at New York-Presbyterian that Zoë slides into this winter, the pixilated imaging on the monitor that shows there are no tumors inside her body. These are the second-year tests, ones where the research on Wilms' tumor suggests higher and higher percentages of survival. We know from Dr. Lee that next year's scans, the third-year tests, are crucial, too. So we have another year of waiting. I walk out of the hospital feeling the usual relief, and thinking more about faith.

Because what do you believe when you don't believe?

When Sendak and I spoke we talked about why we wrote children's books. Did we have a responsibility to write moral and uplifting books? Or were we writing for ourselves. Were children capable of figuring out their world, and smarter than adults gave them credit for? Or were they in need of saving.

I have a first-edition copy of *The Catcher in the Rye* that my mother gave to me, so dark and leathery it looks biblical. I leaf to the part where Holden Caulfield is watching his younger sister ride the carousel in Central Park and has his epiphany: he can't catch her, can't catch the other children, that they fall and turn out okay—"you have to let them do it."

It's the point of Salinger's book, I think, this leap of faith. I wonder if my generation has made this idea our own secular gospel. The belief that we cannot save others. We listened to friends in trouble, maybe gave them a shoulder to cry on, but friends had to save themselves. They couldn't be rescued, or fixed, or even made to show up on time. People just *were*. We had to accept that.

But a child's illness is different. We fight, to use that word I dislike. We battle, to use the other. We attack illness with all the technology and resources we can marshal. We do not have faith that children will fall and be okay. We don't put our children on pyres, we don't just pray. We reach out and we catch them, we do everything we can. *Not* to try to save a falling child would be madness.

Abraham and Holden both had it wrong. The only sane and human response when faced with a dangerous and unfair world is to rage against it, to attack everything that would harm those we love, and to fight for them with a wild and protective fury.

．　．　．

Slabs of ice jostle against one another at the water's edge as I bike up the Hudson. I'm buried under layers of long underwear, socks and gloves, an orange windbreaker. After looping around Central Park I head back along the river and as I'm riding east on Tenth Street a silver sports car swerves into the bike lane and nearly hits me.

"Watch it!" I yell.

Through the window a voice yells back, "Fuck you!"

At the next intersection I roll up beside the sports car—all I can see through the tinted window are sunglasses—and start saying that he almost hit me, that I was in the bike lane.

"Fuck you! You fucking guys are all the same!" grunts the voice.

So in solidarity with those fucking guys, or to prove his point, I start punching the car. Hard punches, *one, two, three*. Starting with the side mirror until it gives way with a crunch and is dangling by a wire and with one more punch the mess of plastic and glass is clattering to the pavement and spinning across the street.

The sunglasses and I stare at each other for a moment—*What's our next move here?*—and then I bolt. I race up Tenth Street, the car revving behind me, and at the intersection the car fishtails around me and the driver jumps out and I dart around him and keep going, past the Sixth Precinct police station, then hang a left on a small one-way street, lock my bike on a smaller street, pull off my orange windbreaker, and start walking.

I walk home through the park as slowly as I can, my heart racing. Tree branches above, ice at my feet, people going about their days, the world turning around me. I don't recognize myself.

Who is this person?

Williamsburg

———— ∽ ————

I am at Blue Bottle in Williamsburg. The Bay Area coffee company opened a new café here last month, but with its crafted wooden beams and brick façade, the place looks like it's been here much longer. In the back of the café, a roasting machine rattles away. In the front, the glass-paned garage door has been pulled down to keep out today's chill—the kind of spring day still holding on to winter.

I biked to Brooklyn this morning to work on ideas for a children's book, but I find myself distracted so I watch the people in the café and sketch their beards instead. I start with the beards of the baristas. Wispy goatees, scraggly muttonchops. With their short-brimmed hats and denim button-downs it looks as if they had been brewing coffee at a Sierra campground in 1854 and through a trick of time were now pulling espressos in North Williamsburg.

Next I sketch the beards of the men in line. As I draw I come up with theories (the shorter the man, the bigger the beard), and then I start getting annoyed. All these hipsters and their poses. One man looks like a biblical prophet who has a beard trimmer. The woman with him sports yoga gear and a hieroglyphic tattoo on the nape of her neck. Four guys wearing ironic T-shirts just started a coffee "cupping" behind me and the sound of their slurping fills the café.

I think of something said by a father in Mia's ballet class, a schlumpy guy named Louis. In one of his sets Louis C.K. talked about young single people and how their cares—the light in their apartment, or their music collection—just didn't matter when compared to the cares of parents. So as I look at these hipsters I feel I'm seeing them through Louis C.K.'s eyes and I start thinking, *None of you matter.*

The prophet with a beard trimmer takes a seat next to me. He's telling his yoga friend about the dinner he had last night, a slow-braised pork shoulder. Are you serious? When something serious comes into your life, you are more serious. Now he's talking about some place that only uses reclaimed wood, and as I eavesdrop and take notes my annoyance slides into dislike. What are you waiting for? You have time for your beard but you cannot escape life, and you cannot escape death, and just as I'm thinking these thoughts a man walks through the door with what looks like a miniature banjo.

Who *are* all these people? These are end-time people,

with end-time cares and small-time art projects, and everything these people represent adds up to something that

"that" is the word I am writing in my notebook when my phone rings. It is 11:58 on a Friday morning and from the air in Elise's breath, before she even says one word, I know that Zoë's scans are clear and that everything is okay and I walk out the door to the street.

Elise is telling me about their visit to the hospital but I am floating above the street, ten feet in the air, and the sun is steaming the wet out of the pavement beneath me and I am only brought back to ground when I hear Elise's voice again.

"Okay?" she says.

"Okay," I say.

I open the door to Blue Bottle and walk back inside.

And everything is different. As if air has been added to the café, its volume expanded. I know in these fever-breaking moments that my senses are too impression-able. But the people here begin to look different, too. Because these men and women have their own worries. A mother who died, a friend who is ill, maybe one of them had cancer. All that is hidden and unknown. Even if they don't have particular heartache, just the anxiety of being young in the city. Striving and unsure. The worry that in my distraction and lack of empathy I wasn't able to imagine.

Maybe I missed something else. The cares of others can seem ridiculously small (*banjo music!*). And yet, maybe the small speaks to something larger. A wood beam, a hand-sewn dress, a carefully brewed coffee—each one a response to life's uncertainty. An attempt to control what can be controlled, to make one thing as well as possible, and there's something beautiful in that. The beauty of a slow-braised pork shoulder.

I get back in line and order something small and caffeinated. I don't think I will work on a children's book today. Maybe I'll grow a beard. I pull out a worn copy of the book I wrote about being a father and read that instead. It doesn't take long. It's short and upbeat, though there's one sentence about not wanting to become the parent of a child with cancer that makes me suck in my breath.

I look at the line of people waiting to order. More men with beards, more women with tattoos of birds. They still seem fairly silly, but more endearing somehow. Instead of campers from the Sierras, or prophets from the Bible, maybe they're a gathering of Tolstoy's interns. As I look at them standing in line, a line that is now bending out the door, a line so long it cannot make sense, it strikes me that no one is here for the coffee.

The line says we're here for something more. Connection, warmth. A word from a barista, a smile from a stranger, a moment in which we are seen and taken in. We are alone. *We are not alone.* Humans are gatherers, in that we gather. Where by being around others our worries are eased. This is true of a church in Alabama, a diner in South Dakota, or a café in Brooklyn. It's why we walk through the door.

My book *Farm* comes out and we throw a party at our apartment. Friends and librarians and publishers, along with the man who reviewed a previous book of mine in *The New York Times,* and not so well, but he doesn't seem to remember. We set bread and cider on our table, and Zoë and Mia pad around in bare feet, smiling up at the adults.

I throw myself into the book's publication. Bookstore signings, readings at schools, a talk with booksellers at the Eric Carle Museum in Massachusetts. I take my editor and designer out to dinner to thank them, but both are on diets so I finish both their dinners, the most gluttonous and expensive meal I have ever eaten.

When not promoting *Farm* I drive to my parents' farm and sketch their old dog for a book about a dog who sits on a porch. I send sketches to my grandmother, and she sends me letters in her scratchy arthritic script.

The spring expands and I pick Zoë and Mia up after school with two of their friends. Zoë's friend has been her best friend since kindergarten; Mia started school at PS 41 this year and brings one of her many new friends. The girls rumble and swerve on their scooters down the sidewalk in front of me, improvising ballet and gymnastic poses as they go.

At the river we take a right and roll to the playground at the Twelfth Street pier. The playground has a sprinkler. As I hold up a towel, the girls slip out of their clothes and into swimsuits, then after a quick lathering of sunscreen and the barest of waves, they're off.

When I think back to the winter it is with shame. What kind of person punches a car? When I told Elise afterward what I had done, I couldn't explain myself. How wrong to take my fear about my daughter's cancer and turn it against a stranger. How wrong even to blame what I did on being the parent of a child with cancer. As if I were the only person who had ever experienced this. An angry island.

Zoë and Mia come back to me, wet and babbling about some story I can't quite follow. I smile and nod and give them a few dollars for ice cream sandwiches, and they're off again, back into the playground and their world.

Change can come in an instant. A fall, a phone call. Change also comes in increments. Small steps, added over time. From that morning in Williamsburg, and the many mornings after, I hope I may start to see that even in our most isolated moments of helplessness we are connected. Out of islands, archipelagos.

Here I am, looking across the water. On the opposite shore is the Hoboken Terminal. A rail station and a ferry hub, with brick arches and LACKAWANNA in white letters against the brick, a tower rising above the terminal with a round clock face and a blinking light. It's a place of embarkation, and as I look across the river I imagine the far side of the station, with trains heading westward across the rest of the country, over farms and plains and prairies, out into the infinite and the possible.

Remember

———— ✿ ————

Above our kitchen stove is a watercolor of Bolinas Bay, the sheltered estuary north of San Francisco. Heather-green hills shrouded in fog fill the painting's background, on the right is the blue of the estuary, in the foreground there's a white farmhouse in a yellow meadow. When I drew this I was standing by the side of a road looking across the meadow. Not far from me, out in the grass, was a bird.

It was a great blue heron. Head bent, one leg raised. Motionless. As I sketched, the heron lurched forward and speared something with its beak. Then it took flight and began laboring its way across the meadow and as it flew I could see that the something was furry and wriggling. A mole probably. The heron and the mole were fifty feet in the air and heading toward the water when I heard a shriek, and a hawk, wings at its side, dove out of a clump of trees and slammed into the heron. The heron let out an indignant *scqwaak*—wings and legs a-jumble—and the mole fell from its beak. This was all happening quickly, but also slowly, in a sort of suspended state with each detail etched, and as the mole fell toward the ground, another hawk—it must have been the first hawk's mate—swooped in from the other side of the meadow and caught the mole with its talons just before it hit the ground, then flew away.

I went back to my drawing.

Both hawks were gone now, and so was the mole. The heron was beating its furious way back to the bay. The field was deserted. I remember thinking, *That was crazy. That did not just happen.* But, it did.

When I tell this story I think first of the mole, because how wild would that have been to be burrowing in a tunnel, then skewered by a beak, then up in the air, then falling through the air, then caught and eaten. What a way to go.

But this story also makes me think about how we remember. Memories are unreliable as it is, malleable and messy, and become more so with time. This story of the heron is true, but I have told it so often I wonder what I am actually remembering. That foggy morning in Bolinas, or the last time I told the story in Manhattan? When memories are great, I think we remember the retelling. We heighten the dramatic and edit out the mundane, smoothing everything into one story. But what do we do with painful memories?

I wondered this last month after Zoë and I returned from the hospital. Her scans were clear, and after lunch in the Village we met Elise and Mia at a place that makes goat-milk ice cream. As we stood on the sidewalk with our cones, Elise's phone rang. It was Dr. Lee. The day was very hot, but there was a frozen moment standing there where I could tell from Elise's tone that something was wrong with Zoë's scans. A shadow.

Everything turned out fine. Zoë had a cold, and phlegm in her lungs had clouded the X-rays; she went back to the hospital a week later to be safe and her scans were definitively clear. But that moment on the sidewalk threw me backward, with shot-in-the-gut remembrance, to when Elise called me that morning in Chicago, and we met near the park and held each other and tried not to show emotion to the girls, where each sentence we said was deliberate, with appointments and procedures carefully discussed, though nothing we said or did not say could in any way hide what we both felt: terror.

Painful memories have searing specificity. We scald our fingers on a stove when we are toddlers, experience heartbreak when we are teenagers, learn our child has cancer when we are parents, and these memories burn when we remember them. The research on memory points to findings we instinctively already know—we remember pain better than pleasure. Bad memories stick (whereas it can be difficult to recall a pleasant evening with friends, let alone the name of our second-grade teacher). So how do we make good memories stickier, and painful memories less raw?

Maybe we start by reconsidering photography. Recently I was looking through photographs I took when we lived in Chicago: the girls at the zoo, at the greenmarket, on the shores of Lake Michigan. The smiling and interchangeable photographs of any family. I forwarded through these and here we are in the woods of northern Wisconsin the spring before we moved to New York, bouncing along a dirt road in the back of a jeep, Zoë and Mia grinning out at me. Zoë looks so healthy it is breathtaking to look at this photo now and know a tumor was growing inside her. Two weeks after this photograph she will be in surgery.

Then, nothing. As I held down the slide-show button on my computer my photographs stop. I stopped taking pictures. This response may have been drastic, but there's a divide between our lives and the images we use to portray them. We're always smiling when we look into a lens (we rarely photograph ourselves in tears), and we often don't even look at these images afterward. But life can't be this fantastic. All this happiness clouds our memories.

This is why I love to travel. When we travel we are more porous, more open to experience. Experiences are not always good (travel gives us plenty of stories of disaster), but they are concentrated. Stronger memories are created as our other senses take over. The smell of eucalyptus trees in California when I was ten, the sound of country music on my car radio in Louisiana when I was twenty-four, the feel of wind on my skin after I lost my stuffed raccoon on the moors of England when I was five. Years later I hear the same song, or smell the same trees, and that first moment comes rising back. From inside me, where it had been rooted. This rootedness takes place because of how the memory was first planted. I think I was able to remember that heron in Bolinas because I was on the road with a sketchbook and didn't have a camera. Our eyes open when we travel, other senses follow, and the experience enters us and becomes cellular.

Travel, and our memories of it, is also something we give. That's my hope when I travel with my daughters. That the taste of gelato will be more than taste, that its sweetness will carry them back to that piazza in Florence and they'll hear the beep of a passing Vespa and feel the heat of an Italian summer, all combining so that years later they may remember how it was to be traveling with their family when they were young.

Traveling gives memories intensity, but we don't have to travel. Daily rhythms create memories. Walks to school, breakfasts around the kitchen table. This is why I take my daughters to cafés after school, and we drink hot chocolate, and sit in the same seats and look out the same window. Our days accumulate.

Painful memories, like seventh grade, are unavoidable. I don't know if we can ever unremember the bad. The memory of that phone call in Chicago, and the memory of the ultrasound room at New York-Presbyterian, will always stay with me. But maybe our good memories can sit next to our painful memories and watch over them. Cushion them, and soften their jagged edges. Good memories hold us. We create them every day by walking out the door or looking across a field. Surely time and forgetfulness help, too, but I like to think we are protected by the memory of chocolate.

Sometimes I think we *are* memories. I mean, humans are memories. We are the stories we tell and the experiences we share. In what must be the greatest miracle of chemistry, we are able to enter into the memories of those we love. We burrow into them, down into their cells. In this way I hope I can nestle into my children, into the smallest part of them, and will always be with them.

At the end of the summer after Zoë turns eight we drive to Maine to a camp on a lake near the Canadian border. I came here as a boy, and always as summer turned to fall. Warm days, cold nights. A time that looked both forward and back. Before we drove home each year I would jump in the lake and make a resolution, picking one word to say as I leapt. If I was getting ready for the football season the word would be something like "hustle," though in recent years the word has been "clear."

I brought Elise to this lake after we met. It mattered to me that she liked it as much as I did. We came throughout our twenties before the start of the school year. One summer as we canoed in the middle of the lake I asked her to marry me.

Zoë and Mia come with us now. We do many of the things I did when I was young. We swim naked, the water tingly on our skin. We kayak to an island and pick blueberries, though there aren't as many as there used to be. We see a bald eagle. We see waterfowl. We look for moose at the water's edge though we have yet to see one. In the evening we eat hot dogs and baked beans and ice cream. I build a fire while Elise reads to the girls, who curl in blankets and listen. The smell of burning wood spills out the cabin's chimney into the evening air. The sun dips over the mountains, turning the sky into pink ribbons. We hear the call of loons. Shooting stars almost make sound as they cleave the cold black night.

I spread all this out for my children, as if I could fill them. The morning before we drive home we walk down to the wooden pier that sticks out into the lake. Across from us we see the eagle perched in the branches of its tree. A flock of Canadian geese glides by in the shallows, readying to fly south, and farther out is a family of loons. The sky is so big here.

We jump in the lake one last time, and as we wrap in towels I put my hands on my daughters' backs and point out a solitary shape beating its way across the water.

Look, a bird.

Laughter

———— ✺ ————

I am in great shape. I am in *great* shape. I am in such great shape I decide to take the NFL's conditioning test—three sets of twenty back-and-forth thirty-yard sprints—which, incidentally, is named the Cooper. When I ran the Cooper ten years ago I did it in the same time as an average NFL wide receiver, which made me pretty proud.

Over the summer I joined a competitive ultimate game in Brooklyn, and with my ankle fully healed I have been playing hard and fast. So when I bike up to the fields of Central Park to run the conditioning test, I am feeling confident. I'm wearing my favorite shirt, a triumphal red Wisconsin Masters ultimate jersey, and after pacing out the yards and warming up, I start to sprint.

As I make the third turn and reach to touch the ground, a bolt of pain enters my spine. I lurch two feet, keel over to my right, and go down in a heap. As I lie in the grass I think how throwing out one's back must feel like getting stabbed, and how I sprinted into that turn like a stud in a Gatorade ad and came out of it like an old man tumbling onto a sofa.

Once I stagger to my feet I bike home and take all the ice out of the freezer and spread it on the floor and lie on top of it. That evening I receive little sympathy from Elise and the girls, especially after I tell them what I had been trying to do.

"What were you thinking?" they say, shaking their heads.

Toby is more sympathetic and arranges for me to see his acupuncturist. I have never had acupuncture before, and I'm not sure if it helps, but I know that when I tell Zoë and Mia that I had been lying naked in the dark with needles in my back and got an itch on my rear but could not scratch it, that made them laugh.

Nothing makes me happier than making my daughters laugh. Maybe it's how they look—eyes flashing, cheeks dimpling—as if their bodies had been taken over by delight. So at dinner I tell them stories I hope will get this reaction. Something I saw, preferably something gross. Like the one about the red-tailed hawk I saw perched on a branch in Washington Square Park, eating a rat and dropping the rat's guts, barely missing two NYU students texting below on a bench.

It's not just funny stories. I feel responsible for Zoë and Mia's humor education: comics, cartoons, jokes. On our walks home from school this fall we've been stopping at Three Lives & Company and buying every Tintin and Asterix comic, then reading on a bench in the park (checking first for hawks), laughing at every pun and pratfall, the characters tripping onto their butts.

A few weeks after throwing out my back—and countless Advils and hot water bottles later—I feel fit enough to bike to Central Park and play in my laid-back ultimate game. I'm relieved to run with no pain, then run fast with no pain, and when a disc is thrown deep I'm able to sprint down the field and leap high above my defender, flipping over him.

As I lie in the grass looking up at the clouds I realize that this is the second time in a month I've been on my back in Central Park, and also that I cannot breathe. Once I can breathe I bike home and take all the ice out of the freezer and lie on top of it, this time on my front. It takes a trip to the hospital and an X-ray to confirm that I broke a rib, though not before that evening when I go with Sean, one of my funniest friends, to a soccer game in New Jersey and he makes me laugh the entire time and I am in agony.

Zoë and Mia are charmed by my broken rib. When I tell them laughing hurts they do everything they can to make me laugh. Especially Mia, because Mia is incorrigible. So in the next days I try to avoid my younger daughter, and I clutch my rib and think about humor.

E. B. White wrote that humor, like a frog, can be dissected but dies in the process. Humor may be impossible to explain. But if this frog were to be dissected, its guts examined, what would we find? There would be word-play and puns, slapstick and broken expectations (or ribs). But what of the deeper reasons for humor, that infamous equation: tragedy plus time equals comedy. Why do we laugh at what makes us cry, and at what scares us?

At the hospital this fall, after Zoë slides out of the CT scan machine, she draws on the walls. The drawings have multiplied over the years. The castle she first drew joined by a herd of cats, along with the dogs and rabbits and hearts drawn by other children. The CT scan machine "donut," once white and sterile, is now plastered with cartoons and stickers. Zoë finds an untouched space on the wall and draws a gymnast swinging on a bar.

We walk back to the clinic and meet Dr. Lee, who tells us the scans are clear, then plays her customary joke of looking into Zoë's ear with her otoscope and asking what she will find inside (Annie in one ear, Miss Hannigan in the other). After they gossip about third grade, we are free to go. As we walk through the halls Zoë gives hugs to nurses she hasn't seen in months, who are amazed at how big she's grown. What a big girl! Everyone is smiling and laughing. I know there's an edge to this laughter, as we would not be laughing if the scans were not clear. But I find it funny that during these last years I have never laughed more.

On a cloudless morning a few weeks later Toby and I do something hilarious, at least to us. We bike from

Williamsburg into Manhattan, stopping at ten cafés and drinking a macchiato at each one. As we buzz through the streets of Brooklyn we nearly topple off our bikes. Why are we doing this? Who knows! There doesn't seem to be any deeper meaning to this. Can't something be funny just *because*?

Toby and his partner Yuko come for dinner afterward. As Elise and I attempt to cook the wacky-looking Romanesco broccoli they brought from the Park Slope Food Coop, Yuko tells us that as a member of the co-op disciplinary board she caught a woman picking individual cloves off heads of garlic. Toby tells the story of our caffeinated adventure. Zoë and Mia stare at the grown-ups laughing around the table (who *are* these people?), but they are laughing, too. We are all giggling like children and I think, *Why aren't there funny old people?* I don't know any funny old people.

Then I drive to Connecticut and meet Maurice Sendak. A warm morning light cuts through the trees surrounding his studio deep in the woods, casting long shadows. Sendak has a hooked cane, an elfin beard, a German shepherd at his feet. He sits in a creaky wood chair and talks with the children's book authors he's gathered today. As he speaks his eyebrows furrow, making him look cross and kind at the same time. He talks about "scrumptious" books he likes, and "fatuous" publishers he does not. About one reviewer he exclaims, "I was so happy when he died!" He's a little outrageous. I like him immensely.

As he thumps his cane against the floor he sprays the word "crap" around like water from a gardening hose, then mentions a former editor he loved. He has the ability to switch from scathing to tender in an instant, within the arc of one sentence. Joking then not joking, his voice near breaking. We listen, rapt. Maybe old people are funny, or maybe it's just Maurice Sendak.

The suburbs of Connecticut flicker past on my drive home. A familiar landscape of village greens and church steeples, white colonials tucked at the end of driveways, brick schools on the outskirts of town with leaf-strewn football fields like the ones on which I used to compete.

When I played football in high school I played both offense and defense. Sometimes when one of us really laid out an opposing player we'd hop around and whack that teammate on the helmet. We hollered and shouted (if Walt Whitman had ever seen a boy lay out another and come up with a shout he would surely have described it as a "barbaric yawp"), and when the opposing player got up, we shouted at him, too. Eyes flashing, teeth bared, grinning like wolves.

I like to think we didn't act this way toward the other team's weaker players. We saved our grins for the other team's meanest guy, who probably had laid out one of us. As he'd limp back to his huddle we'd watch him go with huge smiles on our faces, and there was nothing funny about it.

Humor is a leveler. It recalibrates and restores, evening out what needs evening. It knocks down the proud (like the pride of someone giving himself the NFL conditioning test) and raises us up. More often, it raises us.

So maybe I laugh when I walk the hallways of the hospital because inside I am scared. Or I laugh as I bike through Brooklyn drinking macchiatos because I worry I won't be able to act foolishly as I grow older. Or I catch myself grinning at players who try to cover me in ultimate and it has little to do with the other guy and more to do with my sadness that I will not be able to run forever.

Maybe, too, the humor of Maurice Sendak, his honest and touching humor, was that of an older man at the end of his days raging against the uncertainty of life. I can't be sure, of course, but I think he was shaking his fist at mortality. Shaking his fist at death.

I don't know if there is anything funny about death, or getting older, the fact that our bodies fail and fall apart. But I do know it is hard to be scared by something you are laughing at. In fact, I believe it's impossible.

The last day of the girls' soccer season, a wet and windy day in late November. Gray clouds hang low over the Hudson, almost touching the top of Pier 40. Inside the dilapidated buildings of the pier are two ragged turf soccer fields; on the roof of the building, next to the nets of the trapeze school, a smaller turf field where the girls play.

Mia is the team's forward. A deft dribbler, she's developing a lethal shot. Zoë is the team's midfielder. She tracks everywhere, always the last girl back, and feeds passes up to her sister. Their teammates are similarly little and quick, and have been running circles around teams of larger girls all fall. They're fun to watch, this team of small girls, a testament to their tenacity as well as to the skill of their coach, Elise.

I am the assistant coach, which means nothing. But for this last game the coaches play, too. Elise and I stay to the sides, passing the ball to the girls when it comes our way. But the coach for the other team is all over. Demanding the ball, shouting at his team when they mess up, only passing to his daughter and yelling at her to *"SHOOOOT!"* The man is hustling against eight-year-old girls: a parody of a coach. He has a ponytail.

After ten minutes of this the girls on our team look at us with frustrated expressions. Elise says something to the coach, which changes nothing, then looks across the field at me. What should we do?

In a moment of perfect timing, the ball pops into the air. As it hangs above us I run toward it, and as I get closer I sense in my peripheral vision a speeding ponytail. The coach and I both are going for the ball, and as we collide I lower my shoulder and push my legs forward—with years of playing football and the knowledge of converging bodies behind me—and I drive through him, his feet spiraling over his head like a comic book villain.

It's a clean hit, though maybe not in soccer.

After helping him off the ground (sort of) and apologizing (not really), I think that sometimes a flattened coach with a ponytail is just a flattened coach with a ponytail. Funny *because*. I also think I'm giving my daughters a story for later, though probably they will be laughing at me for telling it. It's hard to know the guts of humor; part of this was just me being mean. But after I leveled the coach, the game changed. He stopped yelling and started passing.

Humor is not always pretty, or even funny. Humor may not even be humor. It may just be saying something true. But we use it to shake our fists at all that scares us, and with our laughter the world regains its balance.

I'm not sure if we can laugh at all the sadness that inevitably comes into our lives, but do we have a better response?

Thanks

———— ∽ ————

Years ago on a brutally hot day I was driving in the Golan Heights next to a minefield. I had come to Israel with the idea of writing a book, a project that never came to anything following the second intifada. After a few days in Jerusalem sketching sights like the Temple Mount, I rented a car and drove north through the lush green valley of the Galilee, then up to the rubbled plain of the Golan. The landscape was rocky and blistering; a haze lay flat on the horizon. To the east was Syria and to the west was the minefield, which I knew because every quarter mile there was a bright yellow sign that read MINEFIELD.

Israeli army forts rose every few miles. Earth mounds with antennae and netting, and probably guns under the netting, so well camouflaged that at times I couldn't be sure if the mound was a fort or just a rise in the topography. To see better at one point I had to stretch my body across the passenger seat and crane my neck, which kept me from noticing that the car was veering off the road and by the time I did notice, the wheels were catching gravel on the shoulder and the car was swerving back across the road. I froze. My foot stayed stuck to the accelerator and as the car leapt into the minefield the only thought in my head was, *This is going to be really messy dealing with all the paperwork at the rent-a-car place back in Tel Aviv.*

An explosive crunch of rocks rattled the undercarriage as the car bounced through the minefield and at some point my brain came back to me and I turned the wheel—foot still on the accelerator—and the car jumped the shoulder and returned to the road, leaving a smear of rubber I could see in the rearview.

I drove for five minutes. Then I stopped and got out and sat down by the side of the road. I felt sort of shimmery. Blessed, dumb, and lucky all at once.

The relief I felt in the Golan Heights is small compared to the feeling I have each time Dr. Lee tells me that Zoë's scans are clear. Even today, three years after the end of Zoë's chemotherapy, with scans we expected to be clear, my relief is immense. These are the three-year scans, the ones where the research on Wilms' tumor rise to a numerical cure. The scans that answer the question, *Will it be okay?* Yes, *it* will. There will always be worries and this will always be part of her life, but my daughter will be okay. We are done.

As we sit in Dr. Lee's office, with Elise on the couch next to me and Mia wedged between us, I am listening to Zoë tell Dr. Lee about her routine on the bar in gymnastics. Oh, I am not. I am riding this relief, I am coasting on it. I know when we leave the hospital I will pick Zoë up as we walk to the subway and tell her I love her. The train will carry us downtown and we will eat lunch, and Elise and I will call our parents and our friends in Chicago and California and New York. Then I will walk to Three Lives & Company and tell Toby, and if Elise takes the girls for the afternoon I may take the subway to Brooklyn.

The winter day will be bright and there will be an inch of air between my feet and the ground, and when I enter Blue Bottle I will want to hug everyone. I will also want to thank them. Because, as I sat by the side of the road in the Golan I felt not only the relief of an averted disaster, I felt gratitude. Thank God, thank fate. I couldn't wait to find a phone and call everyone I knew—my parents and my friends and Elise—and let them know what they meant to me. But, in a dreamlike turn, I also had the urge to thank people I *didn't* know. The factory workers in South Korea who assembled my rent-a-car, the engineer who designed the road, the creator of gravel.

So after thanking the barista for making my coffee, I will wish I could reach backward in time and thank the researchers who devised doxorubicin, the panels of doctors at the National Science Foundation who designed Wilms' tumor protocols, the construction workers who built New York–Presbyterian, the parents of children with cancer who were not as fortunate as mine. Inventors of antibiotics, designers of stuffed tigers. All those whose commitment and care over the years channeled into our efficient surgeon in Chicago, the cheerful radiologist at Northwestern, the calm nurses in the oncology clinic. People who make me believe we are more protected than we know.

There are times when the brutality of the world, all its horror and injustice, if added together would make us throw our hands up in despair and we would fall apart. But maybe, looked at another way, if all the beauty in the world were added together, each held hand and act of kindness, we could fill with so much joy it would be uncontainable. Humans can be *so* good. Stunning in how good we can be. We can't be so full all the time—our chests would burst—but I think in those times when we are almost overcome by helplessness, we can throw our hands up and give thanks and see that we are saved by others.

My daydream is flying now, back to the moment when a love of learning must have sparked inside a young girl in a small town in Upstate New York, and how that learning grew through college and medical school until that girl became a woman and a doctor, and how that doctor became my daughter's doctor. How that girl saved my girl.

As I picture Dr. Lee—I am seeing her and not seeing her and she's right here in front of me and the thanks I have for her is immeasurable—my daydream comes back to rest, to this small room in this large hospital, and I look at my family.

Zoë is still telling Dr. Lee about gymnastics, her legs swinging back and forth as she sits on the examining table. Mia has clambered onto the table to be next to her sister and is waiting her turn to be heard by the stethoscope. Elise is with me and beaming at our daughters, and at some point Zoë looks over at me and asks me why I'm crying.

"Because he's happy," says Dr. Lee.

Maybe that's true, though "happy" is a small word for what I feel. This sense of landing. It's almost as if I have been forgiven. That I did, as a father, all I could have done. Even if all I have done, the only thing I ever could have done, was bring my daughter to the hospital.

We pack to leave and say our good-byes. Zoë gives Dr. Lee a hug, and Mia gives Dr. Lee a hug, and Elise gives Dr. Lee a hug that fills the room. As we walk out the door it is my turn and I turn to Dr. Lee. I want to tell her so much more—and I suspect she knows this—but all I do is take her hand and say, *Thank you.*

And

———— ✑ ————

My grandmother once had a dream in which she was told the meaning of life. So she woke and reached for her notebook, which she kept at her bedside table for just these occasions, and she wrote down the meaning of life, and went back to sleep, happy in the knowledge that in a few hours she would reawaken and know *why we are here.*

When she got up in the morning she could barely contain her excitement and anticipation, and she rolled over and opened the notebook. There, on page after page, in swirling lines of charcoal pencil, considered from every perspective great and small, were countless drawings of turnips.

Turnips, the meaning of life.

My brother tells the turnip story when we gather to bury my grandmother's ashes at our parents' farm. We are standing in a circle under an apple tree at the crest of the orchard, with spring grass at our feet and apple buds on the trees above us. I dig a hole in the ground and pour my grandmother's ashes inside, placing one of her sable watercolor brushes on top.

My grandmother was a wonderful painter but she was also a sculptor, working in clay and marble. On the table by the front door of our apartment we have a terra-cotta statue she made of three women holding hands. When I look at this sculpture, and consider art that lasts, I can't help thinking that with my watercolors I am working in the wrong medium.

I wonder if all art is an attempt to last. The declaration that *we were here*. A brushstroke by Picasso, a chord by Beethoven, a dance by Martha Graham. It's probably why we painted on cave walls. A few blocks from our home in the Village is a mural by Keith Haring. It runs along the wall next to the pool on Carmine Street where I take Zoë and Mia to swim in the summer. Dolphins and wild sea creatures in thick and animated lines. It's a moving piece, and because of it I have been talking with the librarian at our local library about painting a mural of animals on the walls of their children's reading room. But even sturdy arts are impermanent; Haring's mural has started to chip and fade.

A royalty check for my book *Farm* comes in the mail. It's small, but big for me. I once heard of a writer who complained to a friend that his book had sold only two thousand copies, and the friend replied that if the two thousand people who had read the writer's book walked through his kitchen, all of them shaking his hand, he would break down in tears at how fortunate he was to have touched so many.

I like that about words. How words written by one are received by another. Made in Los Angeles, read in Rhode Island. Crossing borders, crossing years. I like how words, as with a speech by Martin Luther King, Jr., can change the world. Words can also change the world of one person. We need only pencil and paper. We make words; they work for us. The words "fight" and "battle" work for some; the words that worked for me were "laughter" and "thanks." I like "beauty" and "hope" too, as they speak to the best in us.

The most beautiful thing about words is that we find them inside us. Accessible within. We have only to dig down to that spot and bring them out. It's as easy, and as hard, as that. We peel down to that layer of ourselves as if we were an onion. Or, a turnip.

I take a train across the country to research a children's book on trains. The train rolls over the Great Plains and climbs through the Rockies. In western rail yards I get off and sketch massive Union Pacific engines, then get back on and talk with fellow passengers in the dining car. My sketchbook fills with drawings and stories. At night the train sways under a constellation-packed sky, and we bend toward California.

The girls fly out and join me. Elise has a conference in San Francisco, and while she has meetings, Zoë and Mia and I ride the cable car to Fisherman's Wharf, clattering and clanging up and down the hills. The girls stand on the sideboards, hands tight on the poles as they lean into traffic, their curly hair whipping back at me. We are unstoppable, the three of us. Afterward we go to Blue Bottle and eat waffles drowned in syrup, then ride the cable car again. Waffles, cable car, repeat. In the afternoon we meet up with Elise and cross over to Berkeley and walk the hills where we used to live. After a few days we fly home to New York.

Zoë is finishing third grade, and Mia is finishing first grade. In the morning we walk them to school through Washington Square Park under trees blossoming in pink and white. Then I walk with Elise to her office before getting on my bike and heading to Brooklyn and the café where I start taking notes for this book.

The seasons change again and on a pretty day in early summer, Elise and I bring the girls down to the river, to the trapeze school on the roof of Pier 40. We say hello to the muscled instructors as Elise attaches a harness around her own middle, then helps Zoë with hers. Zoë wears a pink running shirt with RUN LIKE A GIRL written across its front.

The trapeze class takes turns climbing the ladder to the launching platform, then swinging back and forth on the bar—first with their hands, then upside down by their legs—before dropping into the net below. Mia is too small so she stays with me next to the net, looking up.

After a few practice swings the class is ready for "the catch." At the peak of the swing, with legs hooked over the bar, they will reach out and try to get caught by an instructor swinging from a bar at the other side of the net. Elise goes first. Out she swings, and at the instructor's call she stretches her arms and latches onto the catcher's forearms, holding for a second before flopping down to the net with a grin. The catch looks impossible, until it isn't, and then it is Zoë's turn.

She climbs to the platform. The instructor behind her clips her harness into a safety rope. The instructor on the ground plays out a rope that will guide her forward. The catcher across from her swings back and forth, arms waiting. All these people, all these arms and nets and ropes, watching out for her and keeping her safe. Metaphors are everywhere. She is held by metaphors.

As Zoë takes the bar, everyone on the ground stops to watch this small girl fly. I am looking too, and as I do I feel I am seeing more of her: as an infant, a toddler whose fingers I held as she learned to walk, the girl who came through. In seeing her I am also seeing myself: as a young man with a child, and as a man who is not so young now, watching his child grow.

My daughter sat on my lap at a baseball game in Chicago and it changed my life. She got better, I got worse.

Or at least, different. Sometimes I wonder if I have learned anything since that day four years ago other than that we are all in it. When faced with the impossible, we throw everything we can. Science, love, family, hope. In the end, words. Words that gather us together and let us know we are not alone—with every breath we take and send into the world.

The instructor calls and Zoë jumps, and now she is upside down with her legs over the bar, and at the next call she arches outward, arms reaching and hands searching but her hands glance off the catcher's forearms with a bump. She falls, slowly, down into the net with a stagger and a bounce.

As she lowers back to ground, I can tell she is quietly furious. She's upset she missed the catch and trying not to show it.

But no matter.

I know she will make the catch the second time. I am certain of it. She is so determined, this girl. She has to wait, there are others before her. She stands by herself and looks up. When it is her turn she climbs the ladder, step by step, and when she reaches the platform she takes the bar in her hands. The sky is a brilliant blue. Everything in place. Past and present. Days and years in front of her, the love and hope of those beneath her. She steadies and waits for the call and then the call comes.

And with a bend of her knees, she leaps.

ACKNOWLEDGMENTS

———— ∽ ————

Words can't quite describe the gratitude I have for the doctors and nurses at Children's Memorial Hospital, Northwestern Memorial Hospital, and New York-Presbyterian who cared for my daughter. I hope this book makes that clear.

My thanks to those who helped with the book's writing. To Austin Bunn and Janice P. Nimura, whose thoughtful feedback shaped each draft. To Risa Goluboff for her wise advice, and Barney Latimer for his elegant line edits.

Thanks to the baristas at Stumptown Coffee on Twenty-Ninth Street, where I wrote much of this book. Thank you to the many other cafés in which I wrote, from Blue Bottle Coffee to Café Grumpy—though I found I was also able to write at places like the School of American Ballet and the Antietam National Battlefield.

Thanks to friends Yuko Uchikawa, Richard Schragger, Sacha Spector. Thanks to Joshua Spanogle for our late-night talks. Thanks to Toby Cox, for his daily kindness and our soccer trips to England. Thanks to the staff at Three

Lives & Company. Thanks to my brother, my mother, and in particular my father, who rescued my laptop when I left it on a porch far from home. That was unnerving.

Thanks to my agent Liz Darhansoff, for her years of support. Thanks to my insightful editor, Edward Kasten-meier, and to Emily Giglierano, Deborah Garrison, Amy Ryan, Rita Madrigal, Michiko Clark, Altie Karper, Janet Hansen, Jordan Pavlin, Dan Frank, Sonny Mehta, and everyone in the Pantheon, Knopf, and Random House family whose work turns writing into books. Thanks to my family at Scholastic, too.

Twenty-five years ago I met Elise Cappella when we were sophomores in college. She was tenacious and beautiful then; she is now, if possible, even more so. Thank you for being my first reader, and for understanding that this was something I needed to do. And to my daughters, Zoë and Mia, thank you for giving me permission to write this, and for listening as I read it out loud. You are both excellent editors. This book is for you.

About the Author

Elisha Cooper is the author of *Train, Farm, Homer,* and *8: An Animal Alphabet.* He was awarded a Sendak Fellowship in 2016. His children's book *Beach* won the 2006 Society of Illustrators Gold Medal. *Dance!* was a 2001 *New York Times* Best Illustrated Book of the Year. Other books include *A Year in New York* and the memoir *Crawling: A Father's First Year.* He lives with his family in New York City.

A Note on the Type

The text of this book was set in a typeface named Perpetua, designed by the British artist Eric Gill (1882–1940). Gill derived the shapes of the roman letters from stonecutting, a form of lettering in which he was eminent.

Typeset by Scribe, Philadelphia, Pennsylvania

Printed and bound by R R Donnelley,
Harrisonburg, Virginia

Designed by Betty Lew